THE BUILDING BLOCKS OF MEDITATION

The Purpose of Meditation and

How to Start a Daily Practice That Actually Sticks

NICK KEOMAHAVONG

CO-AUTHOR AND EDITOR
Venerable Michael Viradhammo

ILLUSTRATOR AND COVER DESIGNER
Venerable Tim Dhiranando

TABLE OF CONTENTS

INTRODUCTORY CONTENT

PREFACE

The information within this meditation guide comes from the lens of an American Buddhist monk of the Thai Theravada tradition. I am not a Buddhist scholar. I am not a meditation master. But I am a practitioner of meditation who has learned from direct disciples of my meditation masters. These monks have dedicated their lives to perfecting the art of advanced meditation. Their direct guidance has proven to be incredibly transformative of my own personal practice over the years.

I recognize, however, that most people do not have access to such qualified meditation teachers in such an intimate setting. So, out of gratitude to my masters and my teachers, I wanted to make their wisdom accessible as a simple guide to help new meditators get started off on the right foot. This book combines their teachings with the know-how that I have gathered from my own experience to help you save some time and headaches when seeking to start a meditation practice.

However, if you happen to practice meditation and have already discovered an effective method, this book can still be very helpful for you. The framework laid out in this book will present you with the *universal building blocks* of meditation that can serve to supplement an existing practice. Consequently, following the guidance of this book does not require you to abandon a method that already works for you. If anything, it will provide you with a few more tools to help you still the mind.

And, if you are completely new and have never meditated a moment in your life, this book is specifically designed for you. This book will help you build a strong foundation for a sustainable meditation practice in a very straightforward, simple, and easy to apply way.

This beginner's guide will keep academic and religious terminology to a minimum. It will avoid the use of vague, flowery language that tends to over-mystify instead of clarify meditation. It will also not include tangents of unnecessary personal storytelling that don't directly help you understand what meditation is and how to practice it. Without sacrificing depth or essential information, this book will get right to the point.

It will be an easy read. A concise read. A fun read. And it will help you understand and apply the following concepts to create a better quality of life:
- What is meditation?
- Why is meditation so important?
- What is the mind and what is its nature?
- Why is stillness the key to success in meditation?
- What are some tools I can use to practice meditation?
- Why is it so important to meditate every single day?
- And most importantly: *How do I create a strong daily practice that actually sticks?*

Many of the topics that will be addressed through answering the questions above are very deep and profound. But, following the lead of my meditation masters, I will illustrate such spiritual concepts with relatable analogies that are so simple that even a child could grasp them. This will ensure that the average human with any level of experience or knowledge can properly understand these concepts that are fundamental to building a strong foundation for a meditation practice.

And, if you are looking to deepen your practice after establishing a strong foundation, I am excited to inform you that my team and I have also designed a meditation journal to supplement the information in this book. A meditation journal serves as a powerful tool to sharpen your skills of observation. It will help you discover and clarify your own very specific path to stilling the mind with more depth and consistency. So, if you are interested in utilizing this interactive resource, then please feel free to check out the two editions we have created in both e-book and paperback format. It will certainly serve as a trusty companion as you start your meditation practice under the guidance of this book.

With that, I am very excited to be able to extract the wisdom that I have been fortunate enough to learn here in Thailand and deliver it to a Western audience. I am excited for the benefits that you and those around you will experience as you develop and hone your ability to still your mind in meditation. So, let's begin, shall we?

INTRODUCTION

Good News and Bad News

So, you want to start or strengthen a meditation practice. . . . Hopefully, this is a safe assumption given that you have picked up this book. Well, I have good news and bad news for you. It's always fun to start off with the bad news, so here it goes.

The bad news is that establishing a consistent meditation practice can be quite overwhelming. If you google "meditation" or "how to meditate," you will end up with more questions than answers. You will be met with a barrage of information by various gurus, teachers, traditions, celebrities, authors, yogis, and phone apps all providing guidance in a wide variety of ways.

There is sitting meditation, standing meditation, walking meditation, humming meditation, drumming meditation, and everything else under the sun. Some say to focus on breathing, others on various points in your body. Some say to have your eyes open. Others say to keep them closed. Some are guided. Some play background music. And some are silent. It's all just . . . too much.

This surplus of seemingly contradictory information can create quite a bit of doubt and give rise to a swarm of questions like:

Which one do I pick? Which one is valid? Which one will work best for me and my situation?

And if you happen to overcome these questions and actually start a practice, then you can struggle with some new questions such as: How long should I meditate? How often? What time of day is best? How do I fit it into my busy schedule? Am I doing this right? Is it normal for me to be thinking the entire time I'm sitting? Is it normal for my body to hurt so much?

Oftentimes, people wrestle with these doubts without having access to a teacher or a community that can provide them with clear and consistent guidance on how to overcome these issues. This can lead to them feeling very lost. Without adequate support, the new meditator might just assume, "Well, I guess I'm just not good at meditation," and give up the practice entirely.

Ok . . . so, are you ready for the good news? The good news is: I've been there before. I know what it's like to have the intention to start a practice but also a lack of clarity on where and how to start. That's why I filled this book with everything that I wish I had had access to when I was struggling in the beginning stages of my own practice.

In the chapters that follow, you will be equipped with a very solid understanding of the *universal building blocks of meditation*. The conceptual framework will help clear up any uncertainties or doubts that you have at the moment. It will walk you step-by-step through the process of beginning and progressing down this meditative path and experiencing the fruits of your practice in the form of a better quality of life.

So, I just want to say: Congratulations on picking up this book with the intention of incorporating meditation into your life. This will be the beginning of a habit that is *deeply* transformational.

I want to emphasize, however, that meditation is not only deeply transformational; it is deeply *necessary*. Most of us have never learned this, but meditation is actually an *indispensable* habit to those wishing to live a healthy and well-balanced life.

Shower the Mind

Growing up, we all learned that there were certain activities that should be completed every day in order to look after our health and well-being properly. This includes eating, sleeping, brushing our teeth, and taking a shower.

Let's say you go a day or more without taking a shower. You will definitely start to feel it. And if you don't feel it, you'll definitely start to *smell* it. And so will the people around you. So, for the sake of your own personal hygiene and the consideration of others, we were all taught that it is important to shower every single day.

But what about the mind? We will explain the nature of the mind much more clearly in a section that follows, but, for now, the important thing to note is that the mind—much like the physical body—also gets dirty. From stress, worries, overactive thoughts, heavy emotions, and more, the mind collects many contaminants as we go throughout the day.

But unlike the physical body, the dirtiness of the mind cannot be detected by our sense of sight or smell. But you can be sure that you and the people around you will still certainly notice . . . when your *mood* stinks. For this issue, we can't quite rely on the power of soap or deodorant.

So what can we do to solve this? You guessed it—meditation. In fact, meditation is just like a daily act of showering or brushing your teeth. But whereas your physical body requires a fully *physical* action, your mind requires a fully mental action to clean it properly. Or, more accurately stated, the mind requires *mental in*action.

Meditation is a process by which we detach from our daily mode of thought and bustling mental activity to discover a stiller state of mind. And in this stillness, the mind cleanses itself. Stress, worries, and excess thoughts begin to fade away, leaving behind a mind that is bright and happy. Although this wasn't taught to most of us growing up, this habit is also very essential if we want to look after our health and well-being properly.

So for your own mental health and happiness and for the consideration of those who you interact with on a daily basis, you should shower your mind every single day. This will certainly help alleviate your "stinky" moods.

Book Structure

And luckily for those who would like to overcome such "mental stinkiness," the structure of this book will provide you with simple and focused guidance on your journey to this cleaner, happier mind. Even if you are an absolute day-one beginner, this book will handhold and coddle you each step of the way. Don't worry. We're in this together, my friend!

The book will achieve this end through well-organized sections that provide a balance of conceptual knowledge and practical stepwork. To get an overview of what you can expect to learn, we will take a moment now to briefly summarize each part of the book. The book will be divided into three distinct parts, each containing two chapters that share a central theme or aim. This style of organization will allow you to easily navigate the various sections of this book in the event that you need to come back and review something specific as you progress in your practice.

Part I, which follows this introduction, will help you clearly understand meditation and the mind. This conceptual knowledge will allow you to fully appreciate the value of putting time into developing this meditation habit. Part II will focus fully on the practical know-how necessary to meditate effectively. In addition to using plenty of simple analogies to help you grasp the essence of the three main meditation tools discussed in this book, it will also cover the quintessential body-mind balance that we want to establish when meditating. This part of the book will be very interactive and engaging, as it is chock-full of illustrations and practical steps that you can try out as you read.

The infographic at the end of this part of the book will provide you with a visual summary of the key points of how to meditate. It will allow you to easily reference and review the practical know-how contained within part II whenever you want to quickly refresh your memory.

Part III will give you a to-do list of actionable steps that you can take to jump-start your practice before wrapping things up with some ending sentiments to help you see the bigger picture of this transformative habit. And to support you on your path once you begin, there will be a number of helpful accountability resources following the conclusion. This will include things such as: printable meditation habit trackers, information about how you can find and utilize an accountability partner, and more.

To summarize, this book's structure is designed in a way to help you do two things. The conceptual knowledge is primarily aimed at helping you understand what meditation is and the importance of practicing it. The rest consists of practical tips to help you create a daily habit that actually sticks.

That's pretty much the title of the book, so maybe this seems like a redundant point to make here. But I think it's important to emphasize. Why? Because, in an attempt to stay focused and have you successfully achieve these aims, there is some information that—although important to know at some point in your meditation journey—lies outside of the scope of this book.

Become a Practitioner

Now, you might be thinking to yourself, "Isn't the most detailed and comprehensive meditation guide possible the best thing for me as a beginner?" Well, in my humble opinion, not quite. Firstly, a wealth of information might cause you to get overwhelmed and not finish the book or start the practice. That's the first thing we want to avoid.

Secondly, a comprehensive, conceptual understanding of meditation is very much a secondary goal to creating a daily habit of sitting. Reading a lot and practicing sporadically won't lead to integrating truly lasting benefits from meditation into your life. Even if you happen to stumble across an amazingly deep inner experience during one meditation session, it will become merely a treasured memory if you don't have a habit of showering your mind daily. You won't be able to repeat it consistently.

So with that sentiment in mind, the No. 1 priority and the most important thing—which precedes truly sustainable progress in meditation—is just showing up on the mat every day. Without fail.

It's like if you want to learn how to make beautiful ceramic pots. Yes, it is important that you learn the basics of pottery before slapping some clay onto the spinning wheel and expecting to make something pretty. You need some introductory instruction and some guidance along the way. But do you need to research a detailed history of pottery? Probably not-tery. At the end of the day, you just need to keep throwing clay.

You have to *feel* the unique way in which the clay shifts and reforms in your hands as you apply pressure to it in various ways. You have to *feel* the difference between clay that is too dry or too wet to be considered workable. You have to build those hand muscles and form that muscle memory. And, in general, you have to be willing to make a mess of things many times before you can make something that even vaguely resembles art out of that spinning wet blob of dirt.

Figure 1

But through trial and error, observation, and continuous adjustment, bit by bit you will build your skills of making a beautiful pot. But, in the beginning, you just need to put in the hours getting your hands dirty.

Meditation is the same way. The most important thing is committing to sitting down on that mat every single day and closing your eyes. In the beginning, the results are secondary. We shouldn't look for or expect them. In fact, in order to see results, we should get comfortable and be fully content with sitting and not experiencing them.

Seth Godin, a prolific writer and multiple *New York Times* best seller who also discussed this pottery analogy, illustrates this concept beautifully with the following quote:

"If we condition ourselves to work without *flow*, it's more likely to arrive. We do the work whether we feel like it or not, and then, without warning, *flow* can arise. *Flow* is a symptom of the work we're doing, not the cause of it."

Of course you want to enter a flow state and meditate well. Of course you want to still your mind consistently and effectively. Of course you want to be less stressed. More relaxed. Have more clarity. Know yourself better. And it is certainly possible to experience some or all of these things quite quickly. But the only way to sustain such positive changes over time is to focus less on the results and more on the path to becoming a *true* practitioner.

This term—"practitioner"—is very important. So let's define it. We could define a meditation practitioner as someone who makes a vow or commitment to practicing diligently. It means that you make meditation a priority in your life. You hold yourself accountable and make a conscious effort to slowly but surely develop your ability in the art.

Over time, as you allot a chunk of time to this activity each day, you automatically become more invested. You will naturally begin to seek ways in which you can improve your practice, such as reading books, seeking out support groups or meditation communities, attending retreats, and, in general, just gathering more resources, know-how, and support.

Once you become a practitioner in this way, *then* the good meditations will come. You will find your rhythm. You will experience the deeper fruits of the practice. But, again, don't worry about these results in the beginning. Just focus on a habit of sitting every single day. Then the benefits that you seek, and many more that are not even on your radar, will enter into your life.

And here comes some more good news: You can customize this plan and scale it down to fit any lifestyle. Whether you have multiple hours a day available to commit to this habit or whether you can only spare a few minutes in your busy schedule, anyone can develop a truly sustainable and transformational meditation practice.

Meditation isn't as difficult, painful, or extreme as some people believe it to be. It's not complicated or super mystical. It is not exclusively reserved for the extra-disciplined or ultra-spiritual. People can often have this overly romantic perception of meditation.

The image that might come to mind is that of a beautiful woman sitting on a beach in Bali at sunset, adorned with mala beads and flowers in her hair, sitting effortlessly in full lotus position with a slight smile on her face as she floats off into cosmic bliss . . . and yes, this is indeed a great Instagram picture. But the reality is, meditation typically isn't that dramatic.

More commonly, meditation takes the form of a quick five-minute recharge on your lunch break as you close your eyes in your car before heading back into the office. Or sitting at the terminal while waiting for your connecting flight. Or sitting on the public train on the way to school. Or a mother of three getting a few minutes of peace after she just put her children to sleep.

Meditation is universal. It's not religious. It's for everyone who wants to live a better quality of life. No matter who you are, what you believe in, how busy your schedule is, or how many times you have unsuccessfully tried to implement some type of spiritual practice into your life, this book will help you create a *daily* practice. That. Actually. Sticks. It will equip you with the mentality, the know-how, and the tools to succeed.

And if you happen to already be a long-term daily practitioner of meditation, well done on implementing the consistent habit. You have already overcome the most important hurdle in the meditative journey. However, I would like to ask you this: Given your daily habit, for however long you have had it, have you noticed a plateau in your practice? Or an inconsistency in your inner experience?

Facing obstacles, stagnation, or dips in your practice is a very normal thing. So, even if you have been meditating daily for many years, perhaps the lens provided in this book can help you view your practice in a new, refreshing light. This new perspective could potentially help you move past any stagnation that you are currently experiencing. In addition, it is always helpful to come back and reinforce and refine your foundation.

Keep in mind that even elite athletes who compete at the professional or Olympic level continuously drill and focus on strengthening their fundamentals. Michael Jordan certainly spent countless hours shooting free throws even when he was playing basketball at the peak of his career. Honing your meditation skills is very similar to this process of honing your skills in a sport. Continuous improvement requires a commitment to strengthening your fundamentals.

So, my hope for both the new and experienced meditator is that this book provides you with a guide to start you off and keep you continuously progressing down this path of training your mind. This book combines the guidance from my meditation masters and teachers and from my own personal experience into a simple guide to help save you some time and trouble in your own practice. Although I was very fortunate to have access to my teachers in the beginning, I also wish I had had support in book form that I could reference anywhere and anytime. So here it is.

As you follow and practice this guide, it will enable you to access an untapped inner well of wisdom that already resides within you. After this, once you revisit certain sections of this book, you will understand what is written on a deeper level. Because you have already touched it. They aren't just words on a page anymore. They will be a map of your experience. I am excited for your inner journey to unfold. And I am honored to be a part of it. So without further ado, let's discover the building blocks of meditation.

PART I:
UNDERSTANDING MEDITATION AND THE MIND

CHAPTER 1
WHAT IS MEDITATION

Meditation Is Not for Relaxation

That's right: Meditation is *not* for relaxation. It's also not for reducing stress. Nor is it a practice for being more focused and productive. Now, before you close the book, hear me out for a second. These things are all certainly nice *byproducts* of the practice. But they are not the *main purpose* of meditation.

To illustrate this concept, let's make an analogy. It is very enjoyable to eat delicious food. You can't argue with that statement. But even if the taste is the primary reason why we look forward to mealtime, it is not the *main* purpose of eating. Eating is a process by which living beings get rid of hunger and get energy to sustain their bodily functions. Of course, this isn't a super technical definition, but that's the gist of it.

If you don't eat, you will experience ever-increasing hunger pains, and eventually—if you hold off long enough—you will starve . . . and you will die. The enjoyment of the taste, the socializing often surrounding it, and the art of cooking are all enjoyable byproducts of eating. But they are not the main purpose.

So, that leaves us with the question: What is the primary purpose of meditation? From a Buddhist perspective, the purpose of meditation is to purify greed, anger, and delusion from the mind. This purification process is the most direct way to make progress towards spiritual enlightenment. However, many people who are looking to incorporate meditation into their lives do not have such lofty aims.

Such people often just want to find a practice that will help them more gracefully navigate the day-to-day problems they face in modern life. So in order to honor meditators ranging from those simply seeking more balance all the way to those who are seeking enlightenment, it can be helpful to define the purpose of meditation in a way that both audiences can connect with.

In an attempt to do that, we can say that the primary purpose of meditation is to develop the skill of neutral observation.

Perhaps you've never heard it put this way before. But, in fact, this is just another way of explaining the purification process that is happening inside of meditation. Refined skills of observation are absolutely fundamental, regardless of whether your aims are worldly or transcendental.

Before we get around to why this is the case, let's talk about something else: why people are suffering so much. Nowadays, people are suffering. A lot. If you look at the state of the world, it is easy to jump to the conclusion that this suffering is directly caused by the condition of our external environment. We are experiencing divisive social issues, economic crises, political corruption, pandemic disease, environmental degradation, AI taking over the world, and so much more on a massive scale. Some of these issues are unprecedented and seemingly unsolvable. It can be very easy to get consumed by this darkness and confusion.

These problems *are* real. And they *are* scary. However, there *are* people who can live with these realities and still be genuinely happy and live a meaningful life that benefits themselves and others. This way of living is not a result of an "ignorance-is-bliss" "turn-a-blind-eye" or "I-just-don't-care" kind of approach. Rather, there are those who can be aware of the woes of modern life and still live with a deep inner peace.

Granted, these types of people might be few and far between. But they *do* exist. And it *is* possible for anyone to develop themselves to achieve such a mentality. But first, it is important to see clearly the fact that external problems are not the *root* cause of why people are suffering so much nowadays.

The true culprit resides within the minds of each suffering individual. It is the feelings, emotions, opinions, stories, traditions, cultural norms, family values, personal values, media influence, the influence of one's social circle, transgenerational baggage . . . and the list goes on. This collection of factors makes up the various influences that have conditioned our minds throughout our lives.

Each aspect of our conditioning is like a pollutant that clouds the lens through which we view the world. As a result, our perception gets tainted. We experience reality through the haze of various filters that we have collected. We no longer see ourselves, others, or the world around us neutrally. Without neutrality, each experience that we have further deepens these deep-seated biases that we are often largely unaware of. This distorted way in which we view life is thus out of line with the true nature of things.

This is perhaps the most harmful and pervasive root cause of suffering: the inability to see things as they truly are. From a Buddhist perspective, we call this "delusion," which, along with anger and greed, comprise the three root impurities of the mind. The presence of these three impurities is the root cause of the mind's inherent lack of neutrality.

Greed sways the mind to incorrectly perceive the world through the filter of what it likes and craves. Anger sways the mind to incorrectly perceive the world through the filter of what it dislikes and doesn't want. And delusion shrouds the mind in the darkness of the inaccurate views that we incorrectly believe to be true. We will get into these impurities more deeply in the next section, but for now, just know that the mind must be trained properly in order to transcend its conditioning and purify these root contaminants that stand in the way of clear, neutral observation.

In essence, all of the Buddha's teachings guide us down the path of being able to do two things: see reality as it truly is and take steps towards overcoming our suffering. These two dimensions of Buddhism support each other. Initially, the theory provides you with a framework to help you understand cause and effect more clearly. Then you start to apply this theory using practical steps to train the mind. This application helps to bring the concepts that you just learned to life. As you practice more, you grasp the theory with more depth, progressively developing knowledge of things as they truly are. This deeper knowledge then empowers more wholesome and skillful action. It becomes a positive feedback loop that brings you to deeper and deeper levels of awareness.

This process is called "wisdom development." It is the highest fruit of Buddhist practice and the sole pathway to enlightenment. And as you walk this path towards profound clarity of mind, a happier, more aligned, and more balanced life naturally follows as a result.

So, really, the Buddha was a teacher of perception. And he taught that the most powerful and direct way to be able to clean your lens, uncover your delusions, and see the true nature of things is to practice meditation. So, I'll say it again: Meditation is not for relaxation.

The purpose of meditation is *to develop your skill of **neutral observation in order to see yourself, others, and the world around you as they truly are.***

But don't worry. Through the process of training your mind with consistent meditation, you will undoubtedly become more relaxed, stress-free, focused, productive, and happy.

Stillness Is the Key to Success

Now that you understand the purpose of meditation, the next step is to understand how to reach the desired result. How exactly are we supposed to train the mind in order to develop this skill of neutral observation? In other words, what is the mental state we are aiming to cultivate in meditation?

It can all be boiled down into this one simple phrase:

"Stillness is the Key to Success."

Although this phrase might be simple, its true meaning is deep and elusive. To illustrate the importance of stillness and how it functions to purify the mind, let's make an analogy.

Let's compare the mind to a glass of water. This glass is initially full of 100 percent crystal clear water. However, over time, this water collects various contaminants. The first contaminant comes in the form of a drop of dye. When we add this dye to the water, it starts to change color. Now, when you look through the glass at something on the other side, the object of your observation is seen through the distortion of a filter.

Figure 2

This specific metaphor with the drop of dye illustrates the effect that greed has on the mind. The word "greed" might bring to mind an image of a wealthy corporate executive who uses unethical business practices. However, greed in the context of Buddhism and the mind is a much more fundamental impurity. In fact, it exists within the mind of every individual who is not yet fully enlightened. Simply put, it is a self-centered desire for more.

From wanting more food, money, material possessions, pleasure, status, praise, friends, love, and so on and so forth, greed affects us all to certain degrees. It frames the world in a way in which we seek to gain benefit or get our needs met by the people and the situations surrounding us. The mind is stirred up into a state of greed when experiencing or thinking about something that we like and crave.

Now let's imagine that we take that glass of water and add a flame underneath it until it is brought to a boil. As the water bubbles violently, it is impossible to look through the glass and see things clearly on the other side. This specific metaphor illustrates the effect that anger has on the mind.

Figure 3

When we think, speak, or behave under the influence of anger, we create suffering for ourselves and others. This second root impurity of the mind can be experienced as rejection, irritation, frustration, hatred, ill will, rage, and violence. And again, this impurity is contained within each of our minds to a certain degree. The mind is stirred up into these states as a result of experiencing or thinking of things that we dislike and do not want.

Finally, let's imagine that we take a handful of dirt and pour it into the glass. The dirt immediately spreads throughout the water and obscures everything from view. The previously clean and clear water is now muddy, murky, and impossible to see through. This dirt illustrates the effect that delusion has on the mind. Delusion represents all of the beliefs that we hold about ourselves, others, and the world around us that are out of line with reality. It is a mental darkness that stands in the way of clear understanding.

Figure 4

So as we go throughout our lives, we continue adding more of these impurities to our glass of water. We experience things that we like and want. We experience things that we don't like and don't want. This adds more greed and anger to the mind. And we continue to make false assumptions based off of our clouded view of reality. More delusion gets added to the mix.

As a result of this clouded perception, we experience fluctuating emotions like jealousy, irritation, lust, sadness, excitement, disappointment, and so on in response to what we perceive. These emotions can become quite heavy and overbearing. And all the while, we continue to think, worry, plan, and stress as our mind continues in a frenzy of constant movement. This is like continuously adding more and more contaminants to the mind while stirring up that water like a crazy witch brewing a potion.

Figure 5

So what do we do? Should we try to somehow extract all of the pollutants? Not quite. Instead of actively trying to clean the water, what we do is simply put the glass down. We stop adding contaminants. We stop stirring it. And we just let it sit still without doing anything.

Over time, the water will stop moving and everything that is contained within that glass will start to settle to the bottom. After some time of allowing the glass to be still without stirring its contents, you can pick up that glass and look through it while being able to see things more clearly on the other side.

In the same way, inside of meditation, if we start to detach from all of our thoughts, stories, emotions, feelings, worries, and plans, the filters that cloud the mind will start to dissolve. Our likes and dislikes lose their tight grip on the mind, and it settles into a state of calm neutrality. In this state of still, neutral observation, the mind purifies itself. This purified lens then enables you to see the true nature of yourself, others, and the world around you more clearly. And this enables you to make wiser decisions in your daily life.

So this is why stillness is the key to success.

Figure 6

Accessing the Inner Well

People tend to be able to grasp this concept of stillness intellectually. But in practice, many people still often try to bring a problem into their session and "meditate" on it in order to come up with a solution. This point of confusion is likely caused by the various ways in which the word "meditation" has been used in the West.

Sometimes people will use the word "meditation" to describe reflection. In fact, Merriam-Webster provides one definition of meditation as "spending time in quiet thought." Philosophers, like Marcus Aurelius, even label their writings where they share their reflections on deep topics as "meditations." However, meditation in a philosophical context and meditation in a spiritual context are not the same thing.

In a philosophical context, meditation uses logic. In a spiritual context, meditation transcends logic. In fact, once the session starts, logic must be abandoned entirely if the practitioner hopes to effectively still the mind.

To clarify the difference between these two processes, we can turn to the three kinds of knowledge in Buddhism. This list goes in order of progressive levels of refinement and depth. Each level is more profound than the next.

The first level is knowledge gained by way of learning. Right now, you are reading words in a book. The knowledge contained within these words enters your mind and can be comprehended to a certain level. In addition to reading, this level of knowledge can also be gained by listening to someone speak. This is the most basic level of knowledge.

The second level is knowledge gained by way of contemplation. So, let's say that after you read a section of this book, you put the book down and "spend time in quiet thought." You start making deeper connections between the concepts you have learned and your own experience. These realizations bring the conceptual information to life and help you understand it on a deeper level.

The third and final level of knowledge is knowledge gained by way of meditation. This knowledge can only be accessed by bringing your mind to a standstill and maintaining it at single-pointedness. There is no thinking. There is no reflection. Just pure stillness while maintaining consciousness. And within this stillness lies a deep inner knowing. This state of mind transcends logical processes entirely. It provides you with access to the most profound knowledge available to human beings. And it can only be fully harnessed through training the mind in the proper way.

This last type of knowledge can be compared to a deep underground reserve of fresh water. This water is rich, full of minerals, and of the highest quality. And it is sitting right underneath your property. However, most people don't even know that they are sitting atop such an incredibly valuable resource. If they do know, oftentimes they don't know the proper way to access the source. So, it's essentially like they don't even have that water in their possession at all.

Figure 7

But if you cultivate the ability to properly calm the mind until it reaches a standstill, then it is like being able to drill down to the source and liberally draw from its endless reserves. That pure knowledge—that is of a much more profound quality than knowledge gained through learning or reflection—will flow readily into your mind.

So again, meditation is not a time to actively try to solve your problems. It is a time to let go of those problems entirely, not merely for the sake of a momentary relief or escape from the stress that they can create but for the purpose of accessing this deep inner well of wisdom. Although logic is helpful and necessary to properly navigate and live in the physical world, it can actually become an obstacle in the spiritual world. It stands in between you and that inner well.

Figure 8

In addition, when you can truly let go of logic and touch this space of profound stillness inside of yourself, the resulting mental clarity will greatly aid your problem-solving abilities. Once your meditation is over, you can reapproach the issues you are facing with a more refined perspective. We could even say that it will make your logic more powerful by both increasing your focus and giving rise to revelations and solutions that you never even considered before.

Naturally, if you haven't experienced stillness from meditation before, the idea that knowledge can arise without using logic isn't a concept I'm asking you to accept on faith. Rather, you must practice diligently in order to prove by yourself whether it is true or not. And we will get to the practice shortly.

But, for now, just keep in mind: During meditation, "stillness is the key to success." It is the key to gaining access to that inner well that resides within each of us containing knowledge of the deepest kind.

Figure 9

CHAPTER 2
THE NATURE
OF THE MIND

The Mind and the Brain

Similar to how doctors learn about the nature of the body before learning how to treat it, it is important for you to understand the nature of the mind before you learn how to meditate. Because, after all, the mind is the object that we are training in meditation.

In the West, our culture does not introduce us to this concept of what the mind is and how and why we should train it to achieve stillness. This topic is typically entirely absent from Western education systems. But if we want to be able to properly navigate the many complex issues that we face in modern life, we need to educate ourselves on the nature of the mind and how to train it in this holistic manner.

Now, you might be thinking, "Well that's not the case! We know a lot about the mind. Neuroscience is a rapidly expanding field of study. We now know that we can continue to train ourselves to develop new and stronger neural pathways throughout our life through the process of neuroplasticity. There are plenty of people pursuing higher education, conducting extensive research, and funneling energy and resources into discovering more about this complex organ that resides in our head."

Figure 10

This is all true. However, it is important to note that despite these two terms often being used interchangeably in the West, the brain and the mind are *not* the same thing. As a meditator—and as a human being—it is important to understand the difference between the mind and its physical counterpart. To do so, let's make an analogy. The brain and the mind can be compared to the hardware and software of a computer.

The brain is like the hardware of a computer. The hardware consists of things such as the keyboard, the mouse, the monitor, the wires, the circuitry, and all the other physical components of a computer. The brain is composed of gray matter, neurons, fluids, and many other anatomical constituents. So the brain—like the hardware of a computer—is of a physical nature.

The mind, however, is like the software of a computer. Computer software is a nonphysical program that works in cooperation with the computer hardware. This software enables users of the computer to conduct various tasks. We will cover more details about the characteristics of the mind in the next section.

Figure 11

But, for the moment, the most important thing to understand is that in order to have a functioning computer, you need both hardware and software. If you are missing one of them, then it can't quite be considered a useful machine . . . or a machine at all. In addition, if there are significant issues or malfunctions with either one of these systems, then the computer cannot function at full capacity. Conversely, if you upgrade the software or hardware of a computer, it can function more quickly and efficiently.

The mind and the brain have a very similar relationship. If you suffer severe brain damage, the mind cannot function effectively. On the other hand, if you were to meditate consistently for a stretch of time, it can "upgrade" the functioning of your brain. If you are interested in such things, then you can google "neuroplasticity and meditation." There is a growing amount of scientific research being done in this area.

But the key takeaway from all of this is that the brain and the mind affect each other. An increase or decrease in the functionality of either component will lead to a corresponding change in the other. However, despite being closely interrelated, it still remains true that the brain and the mind are not the same thing.

To further illustrate this point, we can reflect on what happens when the physical and nonphysical parts of ourselves are separated. Let's say you just have a body without a mind. What is this called? You could call that a corpse. Then let's say you have a mind without a body. What is that called? Some would call it a ghost. Others might call it a spirit. And some might just say that it is not a real thing.

And if you possess this last viewpoint, then don't worry. I'm not trying to convince you of anything you don't believe in. But if you don't believe in ghosts, well . . . at least you believe in corpses, so the point can still be understood. The nonphysical mind and the physical body work together like the software and hardware of a computer. When they are fully separated, you no longer have a living, breathing human being.

And one last side-note on terminology before we move on: There are other terms that people use to describe this spiritual side of ourselves such as the soul, the heart, the spirit, or consciousness itself. To avoid confusion, we will not use these terms. "The mind" is the most common term in a Buddhist context, so that is what we will use to describe the nonphysical dimension of our being throughout the entirety of this book.

Characteristics of the Mind

So if the mind is nonphysical, then what are its characteristics and how do we observe them? Glad you asked.

Here is a list of defining characteristics of the mind:
- It is prone to constant movement.
- It can wander fast, far, and wide.
- It is hard to see.
- It is difficult to detect.
- It is unsteady.
- It is excitable.
- It is difficult to control.

If you reflect on your own mind, I'm sure that some, if not all, of the characteristics listed above will resonate with you. As you can see, the mind certainly is not confined to the skull like the brain is. It is constantly traveling, often in the chaotic manner described above.

To illustrate this unwieldy nature of the mind, people often compare the mind to a monkey. A monkey is quite a rambunctious little animal.

Figure 12

It is noisy, jumps around all the time, and is constantly getting into trouble. Monkeys are very temperamental and moody. And they are extremely difficult to control.

If left untrained, this will be the typical mode of operation of our mind as well: flitting about between many different thoughts, emotions, feelings, and other mental states. Perpetually pulled after all of the pleasurable sights, sounds, scents, flavors, tactile sensations, and mental activity that we experience like a moth to the flame. And continuously repelled by any of the unpleasant counterparts of these sense experiences.

Often without permission—or even much awareness—on our part, the mind is stirred up into states of craving or aversion at a moment's notice. Then we get caught in a never-ending pursuit of happiness by chasing all of the people, places, things, and situations that we like and want to have or experience. We get stuck in a continuous flight from suffering by desperately trying to avoid everything that we don't like and don't want to have or experience. Left with a looming sense of dissatisfaction with this endless cycle, stillness and neutrality of mind can often seem like some distant, unattainable goal.

It can seem impossible to disengage from these patterns of mind wandering and mood fluctuations. Because, obviously, we have certainly tried to stop them. But typically, our efforts to forcefully will our mind to stop daydreaming, worrying about the future, or getting pulled to persistent memories while staying rooted and focused in the present moment leave us feeling very frustrated and even hopeless. And that's because sheer power of will is a largely ineffective approach to cope with these mental tendencies.

But don't worry. There is a light at the end of the tunnel—or, more accurately, at the end of this first part of the book. Part II will provide you with all of the ins and outs of a much more effective approach to calming that crazy monkey mind.

Obstacles You Might Face

However, even if you use an effective approach, it is almost an absolute certainty that you will still face obstacles when practicing meditation. But, again, there's no need to worry. This just reaffirms that you are indeed a human and not some divine being.

Meditation obstacles are a completely normal and natural thing. It is simply the nature of the mind to respond with resistance when we attempt to bring it to stillness. But with diligent practice, you can certainly get very proficient at managing such resistance.

So the question is: What obstacles can we expect to face? In a Buddhist context, we typically break down meditation obstacles into a framework called the five hindrances. But, for simplicity's sake, we can reframe the five hindrances into a three-category system that can be a bit easier to grasp and apply. This framework—which I learned from my meditation masters and teachers—is a very effective way of understanding and overcoming meditation obstacles.

The main obstacles that you will face are as follows:
- Mind Wandering
- Tension
- Sleepiness

Mind wandering is perhaps the most prevalent obstacle. This category includes things such as sporadic thoughts, troubling emotions, and feelings such as restlessness or doubt. The next category, tension, can show up in the form of bodily aches and pains or as a mental tension that often takes the form of heaviness or strain in the eyes or muscles of the face. And lastly, sleepiness is relatively self-explanatory; it's a heavy feeling of drowsiness.

Besides this preliminary description of what they are and some general methods to overcome them, this book will not focus on specific techniques aimed at overcoming the many nuanced variations of each category of obstacles. Again, as a beginner, such detailed information can actually take away from your practice. If we focus too much on obstacles that you have not even experienced yet, then it can cause you to overthink. It runs the risk of creating expectations that can become new obstacles in and of themselves.

Once you start a consistent practice and rack up more of those meditation minutes, you will have something tangible to work with. You will be able to form a clear understanding of the nature of each obstacle by experiencing them directly. It is better to learn in this way rather than trying to imagine what each obstacle will be like after reading conceptual knowledge. So although overcoming obstacles is very important for meditation practitioners, we want to focus on getting over the hurdle of becoming a daily practitioner first.

For now, just know that it is common for beginners—and even long-term practitioners—to encounter mind wandering, tension, and sleepiness while meditating. So, when you invariably encounter one or all three of them, don't get disheartened. Just remember that it is normal and natural, and simply bring your attention back to the meditation tools that we will cover in the next chapter.

PART II:
HOW TO
PRACTICE MEDITATION

CHAPTER 3
MEDITATION
METHODS

Finding the Proper Toy for Your Puppy

Now for the moment you have probably been waiting for: How do you actually meditate? How do we bring the mind from its normal state of commotion into the state of stillness that we have been describing? How do we tame that bothersome little monkey mind?

Although the mind is very accurately personified by a monkey, you probably don't have much experience training monkeys. To any professional monkey trainers out there, I apologize for being overly presumptuous. A dog, however, *is* an animal that happens to be quite a common household pet. And even if you are not a dog owner yourself, chances are you are likely familiar with the general process of training a puppy—either from watching your friends or from seeing an actor in a movie wrangle these wild little beasts. So, in order to illustrate how we properly use a tool to still the mind, we will compare training the mind to the process of training a puppy.

One very common and simple way of training a puppy is to get it to stay still. So, what happens when you put the little fluff ball in front of you and tell it to "Stay!" as you slowly walk backwards? Naturally, it does exactly the opposite. It runs around and gets into all sorts of trouble.

So how can we get it to stay in one spot? One option is to give it a toy to occupy its attention. If it happens to be a toy that the puppy likes to play with, then the puppy will sit there nice and still as it gnaws on its new gift. And, of course, this is followed by a "datza goood girrllll" in an absolutely ridiculous voice while providing the puppy with an enthusiastic belly rub.

But what happens if the puppy is not so interested in the toy that you provide it with? Then, of course, it will run away and find something more interesting to play with. So, as its trainer, you have to experiment to see what your puppy's preferences are.

Figure 13

Some puppies like tennis balls. Some like stuffed animals. Some like bones. And others like your nicest pair of dress shoes. Only through trial and error will you succeed in finding a toy that effectively preoccupies your puppy.

Training the mind to be still is very similar to this process of training a puppy to sit still. The untrained mind—like a new puppy—does not respond so well to orders. Have you ever ordered your mind to "Stop thinking!" while it was fixated on some troubling issue? If so, how did that work for you? Not very well, huh?

It is hard for the mind to merely stop and stay still without anything to occupy its attention. As we discussed earlier, it is accustomed to constant movement. So, instead of attempting to force the mind into a state of stillness, we simply give it a "toy." When we gently anchor our mind on a meditation tool in the proper way, all excess thought slowly falls away. As our mind progressively becomes singularly focused on that one object of attention, the mind reaches deeper and deeper states of stillness.

However, just like for a puppy, this meditation tool has to be something that the mind feels comfortable and content with resting its awareness on. And since everyone's mind is different, this is not a one-size-fits-all approach. A tool that works for one person may not necessarily work for the next. Each person's mind has different temperaments and tendencies.

And not only is there a difference from person to person, but our own minds are very different from day to day. Hour to hour. Moment to moment. Our mind fluctuates in moods, energy levels, and so on. So a tool that worked for us yesterday might not work today. One that worked this morning may not work this evening.

So, your task as a meditator is to observe yourself continuously and be able to answer the questions: In this moment, what is the current state of my mind? And which tool is appropriate to still it effectively?

These are questions that I cannot answer for you. Only through very gently giving the "puppy in your mind" a toy and seeing how it reacts will you know what its preferences actually are. Only through consistent practice, observation, and adjustment will you be able to figure out which tool works for your mind in each moment.

Building Your Toolbox

To help you with this training, a solid list of tools to try out will be an invaluable resource. The Buddha actually taught forty different methods to bring the mind to stillness. They range from focusing on things such as the four elements to various colors to concepts such as loving kindness and compassion to some pretty creepy things, such as a corpse at various stages of decomposition.

This last method is definitely not recommended for the faint of heart. But, if you are interested, you can do some further research on your own and look up all forty methods by googling "Kammaṭṭhāna." The Buddha understood the vast differences in dispositions and temperaments of the people that he taught. So, he gave a comprehensive list to tailor to each individual's needs.

But for the sake of simplicity, we will focus on three main meditation methods. Having three methods to experiment with provides you with a good starting point. If you have only one method to start with, then it can feel a bit restrictive. But if you have a list of forty methods to choose from, this can be a bit too broad. Three methods gives you just enough options for experimentation purposes but not a surplus of options that can lead to doubt, indecision, and being scattered and unfocused in your practice.

What we are doing by providing you with these three methods of meditation is essentially like equipping you with a starter's toolbox. As you start a project, maybe a hammer is required. And this works well at times. But there are also situations that call for a saw. And

Figure 14

sometimes you need a screwdriver. There are different situations that require different tools in order to get the job done effectively.

At the beginning, you will be provided with three tools. Then it is up to you to experiment with them to build your proficiency in applying the tools properly. And if you learn a new tool that is not covered in this book as you progress down your meditation journey, then that's great! One more tool in your toolbox!

But the most important thing for now is to avoid overthinking by simply choosing a tool and starting to practice. With time, you will become like a skilled worker with the mind. Whatever situation arises, you will know which tools you have in your arsenal, which one will get the job done effectively, and how to properly wield it in order to bring the mind to stillness.

So with this understanding in mind, let's get into the first tool.

Tool 1: Visualization

Visualization is a practice where you lightly imagine an object within your mind. Some objects that are often suggested to imagine are things such as: a clean, clear crystal ball; a bright shining sun at midday; or a full moon on a cloudless night. These objects are recommended because they are bright, spherical (which is a simple shape with a minimal amount of features to imagine), and are things that most people are very familiar with.

But, if imagining one of these objects doesn't come so naturally to you, you may imagine an image of something you are more familiar with. Perhaps you are a tennis player. Since you see tennis balls every single day, when you think of one, a very clear image easily and naturally pops up.

Or maybe you can easily imagine something that isn't exactly spherical. Let's say you are someone who enjoys spending time out in your garden. So when you think of a rose, an image very easily and naturally arises. That will be just fine as well.

But there is one more piece to visualization that is a crucial point to make. Sometimes people hear the word "visual" contained within the word "visualization" and assume that the most important thing is being able to clearly see an image in your mind's eye. But, in fact, it is not so important what the image is, how clear the image is, or if you even see anything at all.

The essence of visualization is *not* about what you *see* but rather about how you *feel* while imagining this image.

To illustrate this concept, let's do an exercise. Hold your hand stretched out in front of you with your palm up. Now, cup your hand and imagine that you are holding an apple. You just picked this apple up off of the shelf in the refrigerated section in the grocery store. This apple has a certain feeling to it. A coolness. A specific weight in your hand. A smoothness to the skin . . . ok, now I have some questions for you.

Did you see an image when you imagined this apple? If so, what color was it? How big? Was the image very clear or was it just a rough outline? If you didn't see an image, could you at least imagine the feeling of the apple in your hand? The subtle weight, the cool temperature, or the smoothness of the texture?

When we ask people to do this exercise at our meditation retreat, there are typically a handful of people who see an image of an apple very clearly, some who see a vague outline of an apple, some who see a different fruit entirely, and others who don't see anything at all. This is not an exercise to figure out how good you are at visualization. Rather, it is an exercise to let you observe what arises most naturally for you when you imagine an object.

Some people are very visually inclined and can see clear mental images effortlessly. Others are more geared towards feeling. And other people lie somewhere in between. Nothing good. Nothing bad. There is simply a natural tendency of each person's mind when thinking about or imagining something. This exercise is aimed at revealing that tendency.

Figure 15

Whatever you saw or felt, the most important thing that I want to bring your attention to is that this exercise should be effortless. The ease with which you imagined this apple should be a benchmark for the effort that you place into visualization while meditating. If it feels any more difficult, strenuous, or complicated than this, it's a good sign that you are trying too hard.

If it's not such a clear image, we shouldn't try to make it more clear. If we see a pear instead of an apple, we don't need to try to change it in any way. If we don't see anything at all, we shouldn't try to force the creation of an image. And if the image or feeling changes, then we shouldn't try to control it to remain consistent either.

Any of these actions will strain the mind and will often show up—as we discussed at the end of the previous chapter—as tension in the forehead, eyes, or muscles of the face. This is an indicator of too much effort and focus. It's almost as if you are trying to use your physical eyes to "mentally stare" or intensely look at whatever mental image has arisen. And this brings us to an important point. Whenever we see images inside of meditation, we are not seeing it with our physical eyes. Rather, we are seeing a mental image in our mind's eye.

So with that being said, a key point to meditating effectively when using visualization—or really any other meditation tool—is to relax the muscles in your eyes and face. Try to observe whatever image arises very passively, almost as if you are only half-interested in it. Refrain from searching, scanning, or expending anything more than the most minimal amount of effort to imagine an image. And if you notice tension in the eyes or muscles of the face, then simply relax them and reset by visualizing more softly. We will talk more about the ideal amount of effort you should use when placing your awareness on your meditation tool and how to relax your eyes more thoroughly in a later chapter.

But, for now, just know that going with the flow and gently observing whatever image or feeling arises when you imagine an object is essential for effective visualization. The only time we should adjust our approach is if the object of our visualization no longer creates a calm and comfortable feeling when we imagine it. But if it feels natural, effortless, and calming, then just go with the flow. In this way, the object of our visualization will help to gently anchor the mind and slowly discover stillness.

Again, with visualization, it is much more important how you *feel* as opposed to what you see when imagining an object.

Tool 2: A Mantra

Now we move on to tool number two: a mantra. A mantra is essentially a key word or phrase that we mentally repeat over and over again. In other contexts like yoga, mantras can often be vocalized out loud. But for the purposes of meditation, we just imagine this mantra playing in our mind like music in the background.

One powerful and sacred mantra that we use in Thailand is "Samma Arahang." This phrase is in the Pali language, which was spoken around the Buddha's time in ancient India. It also happens to be the language of the Tripiṭaka, which is the sacred Buddhist scriptures of Theravada Buddhism (the type of Buddhism native to Southeast Asia).

The word "Samma" means right or correct. The word "Arahang" means a state of complete mental purity. By mentally repeating this phrase over and over again, it is almost as if we are reassuring ourselves that we are using the right method to reach a state of utmost mental purity.

But the most important thing about the mantra is not which words you use but rather how those words make you feel when you repeat them within your mind. If, for whatever reason, the words "Samma Arahang" do not feel natural or calming to you, or—more commonly—it is difficult to remember this mantra, then you can use whatever word or phrase has the most calming effect on your mind.

Here is a list of some alternative mantras that you can try:
  • Clear and Bright
  • Soft and Gentle

- Let It Go
- Let It Be
- Be Still, Be Calm
- No Need to Explain
- Content, Relaxed, Comfortable
- Neutral, Settle, Standstill

These are just some ideas that you can try out. Perhaps you know another mantra. Go ahead and use that one. Perhaps there is another phrase not listed above that speaks directly to a mental tendency that you have and helps you find stillness. Great! Go with that. It can even be in another language. Mantras of any persuasion will do. If it calms your mind, it'll do just fine.

Figure 16

An analogy to illustrate the function of an effective mantra could be a series of large waves that repetitively sweep over the surface of rough and choppy water. As the large wave sweeps past, it consumes all of the smaller waves on the surface. In the same way, when the mind is turbulent, wandering, and not quite calm and clear, it is much like choppy water. When we imagine a mantra that feels calming to us, it functions like these big waves and consumes the chatter of the mind. It becomes the predominant "thought" that occupies our mental space.

Over time, the mantra irons out that initial turbulence of mind, leaving behind a mental space that is much more still, smooth, and calm. At this point, the mantra might feel unnecessary, in which case you can just let it fall away as you sit and enjoy the stillness.

So, when applying the mantra, just allow it to be a slow, progressive process of ironing out that mental turbulence. No need to be forceful and "mentally shout" at yourself to "LET IT GO!" Rather, we just imagine that this mantra is like some calming ambient music that is playing in the background as it lulls us into a progressively deeper state of stillness.

Tool 3: The Center of the Body

The third tool that we will discuss is the center of the body. Out of the three methods covered in this book, the center of the body is unique in the sense that it is both a tool to still the mind and a destination that the mind will reach on its own when it comes to a complete standstill.

First, let's talk about the location of the center as explained by my meditation masters. The center of the body is a very specific point that you can see depicted in the illustration. We can also try to conceptualize this point through imagination or visualization as well.

Figure 17

To do this, gently imagine a line that enters your belly button and then exits out of your back through your spine. Then imagine another line that enters into your right hip and exits out of your left hip. Now move the point where those two lines intersect up two finger widths from the level of your navel. This intersection point is considered the center of the body. According to my meditation masters, this is the home of the mind where it can access the depths of that inner well of wisdom that we discussed earlier.

Now let's address the fact that, initially, bringing the mind to this point might not be so easy. And that's normal. You can definitely familiarize yourself with this spot by getting in the habit of gently reconnecting your mind with the center throughout the day whenever you can remember.

But inside of the meditation session, many people will use too much mental effort in an attempt to precisely pinpoint the exact location of the center. And as we will get to in a moment, this approach is actually counterproductive. The proper way to arrive at the center of the body in meditation is not through an intense focus. It is not through searching. It is not through forcing.

In meditation, we properly arrive at the center by minimizing effort. We allow the mind to gently rest wherever it feels most comfortable and then just let go. If that happens to be somewhere other than the point that we just discussed, that is ok. When the mind is placed properly at any point and then left alone, it will come to a standstill on its own and will get pulled to the center of the body almost as if it were being acted upon by gravity.

That might sound a bit confusing and strange, so let's make an analogy to illustrate how this happens. We can compare this process to a coin that is dropped into a coin funnel/vortex. As you release the coin at the top of the ramp, it speeds down and enters the funnel and starts to travel around the top edge. As time goes on, gravity takes over and continuously pulls the coin downwards until it drops into the center. All you have to do is let go.

Figure 18

This is similar to allowing the mind to rest at a place where it feels most comfortable. If you do this in the proper way and simply let go, nature will take care of the rest. But when you try to apply force in an effort to search for or pinpoint the exact location of the center, it is like swiping your fingers over the top of the coin each time it passes by. The coin will just continue making revolutions at the top of the funnel. It will never make its way to the center or reach deeper levels of stillness. Too much mental effort disturbs the mind and interrupts its process of coming to a standstill and getting pulled inwards.

So in order to achieve this effortless application of the mind, we simply seek to <u>gently anchor our awareness at a point or in a space that feels easy, natural, relaxing, and creates a feeling of contentment.</u>

If placing your mind at the center of the body does not meet these criteria, you have some other options. Firstly, you could try to expand your awareness so that instead of observing a small point, you are observing the general area of your belly. Perhaps you can achieve this by lightly noticing the rise and fall of your abdomen as you breathe. Or you can imagine an image or feeling in the area of your belly in the way we discussed during the visualization section.

But maybe the belly area simply does not feel so natural for you to observe in any capacity. You might be able to tell that this is the case if you feel a strain in your forehead or eyes while meditating. It is hard to tell—due to your eyes being closed—but this strain typically comes from looking or "staring" down at your stomach in an attempt to bring your mind there.

Since our eye movement is directly linked to where we focus our attention as we conduct our daily tasks, it comes as no surprise that this is a common occurrence for many meditators. But as we covered in the visualization section, it is important to keep in mind that you are not using your physical eyes inside of meditation. Therefore, it is not necessary nor helpful to look or stare at your stomach in order to bring the mind to rest there. But if you notice that your eyes continue to hold tension as they drift and look downwards despite your efforts to allow them to rest and relax, you can simply let go of trying to place your mind at the center entirely. Again, just relax the eyes and muscles of your face and gently rest your awareness at any point in or around your body that feels more natural.

If it feels more comfortable to do so, you can also imagine your mind occupying a space of any size. Perhaps it is calming to imagine that you are sitting inside of a bubble. Maybe that bubble is just surrounding the outside of your body. Or maybe it is as big as the room you are in. Or the building. The city. The world. The universe! Whatever span of awareness feels most effortless and calming in that moment is the right one to choose.

Lastly, it is important not to stress too much about being fully aware of exactly where your mind is resting at any given moment. Sometimes it is difficult to be able to discern this. The truth is: Where your mind is resting is completely secondary to the fact that it is, in fact, at a state of rest and not moving around. So wherever that comfortable point or space happens to be, just let your awareness gently anchor itself there without overanalyzing its precise location or dimensions.

So, you can experiment with lightly anchoring your awareness in various points or spaces and see which of them works best for you in that moment. If done correctly, there will be no desire to change your approach because it feels *just right*. Then all you have to do is let go and let nature do the rest.

Be Patient With Your Puppy

Congratulations! You are now equipped with your very own starter's toolbox containing three brand-new tools. Before we go over the specific ways that you can balance your body and mind for meditation, let's talk about how you should treat your puppy while training it with these new "toys."

Always keep in mind the nature of a puppy when approaching meditation. Of course, our goal is to be able to train the puppy so that it sits and stays in one spot. But as we discussed earlier, puppies often have other plans in mind of a more mischievous nature. Despite giving it such a nice toy that it liked yesterday, there will be moments when the puppy just isn't interested and does not cooperate.

So how should you respond in such a situation? Get angry and scold it? Or sigh an irritated "uuggghhh" as you put it back in front of you and insult its intelligence a bit? Well, hopefully that's not how you react. In addition to being very cruel, this approach will be very ineffective.

Although animals typically do not understand words, they can easily pick up on the energy you bring to the table. So training a puppy in a rough, harsh, or impatient manner will only succeed in stressing it out. In fact, it may grow to become an aggressive, disobedient animal as a result of your efforts. But if you speak to it in a very soft tone and consistently bring it back in front of you, the repetition and kindness will eventually lead to a well-trained pet.

Figure 19

The mind also requires such training with a similar approach. All too often, new meditators will bring some quite lofty expectations of themselves into meditation. Keep in mind, you might be forty-five years old in the physical world, but if this is your first time meditating, you are only one day old in the spiritual world. You might be an adult, but your mind is still just a puppy. So, it is important that we train it as such. Patience and kindness are necessary when attempting to unlearn many years of allowing your "puppy" to run wild and free.

As we first start out with our meditation practice, our mind is not yet familiar with the process of becoming and remaining still. So, naturally, when you attempt to apply a meditation method to discover stillness, the mind can act just like a puppy. It doesn't obey. It wanders. It gets sleepy. It can't quite grasp and effectively apply what you're trying to get it to do. And if it does happen to find stillness, it often isn't long before it's off to the races again.

It can be easy for new meditators to get frustrated with themselves at this point. Many will often pull the mind back to the meditation tool in an abrupt and impatient manner each time they notice that it has strayed. They will allow negative self-talk to surface, such as, "Dang, I'm so bad at this!" or "I feel like I'm wasting my time" or "Here we go again! Why can't my mind just stay still?!" But, just like when training a puppy, this forceful, irritable, and self-critical approach does not lead the mind to being still and calm. In fact, it will just stress you out and, in a worst-case scenario, lead to you dropping the practice of meditation entirely.

So in order to avoid this outcome, just remind yourself that it is normal each time that your mind experiences one of the obstacles that we covered earlier, whether it is sleepy, tense, or wandering around. In each instance, just calmly become aware of the imbalance and then gently reestablish the body and mind balance that we will cover in the next section. And with patience, consistency, and a kind and gentle touch, the mind will eventually develop the ability to discover genuine stillness with consistency.

CHAPTER 4

THE TWO PILLARS
OF STILLNESS

By this point, you are now equipped with three indispensable ingredients for meditating properly:

- An understanding of the goal of meditation: stillness
- An understanding of three tools that lead to stillness
- And an understanding of the gentleness with which you should treat the mind

Now it is time to add one last element to the mix to make this foundation of meditation know-how complete. We will do this by elaborating on the proper mind-body balance that will support you on your journey to tapping into that inner well of wisdom.

Regardless of what tool you use—whether it is visualization, the mantra, anchoring your awareness in a place or space, a combination of the three, or a different tool entirely—the following balance is an absolute necessity for the mind to come to a standstill. No matter the method or school of thought, this balance cannot be overlooked.

What balance, you ask? The balance between *comfort* and *awareness*.

Figure 20

These are the two pillars of stillness. Each of these pillars must be present in the appropriate amount in order to meditate effectively. So this chapter will help you understand the essence of each pillar and how to establish and maintain each one properly.

Physical Comfort

For our method, comfort is the heart of meditation. It is, therefore, the first thing that we need to establish. By properly addressing its two categories—physical comfort and mental comfort—the mind will be primed for stillness to arise.

Out of these subcategories, let's take a look at physical comfort first. If the body is uncomfortable, the mind will struggle to reach stillness. So physical comfort must be addressed before we move on to anything else.

And let's be honest. Meditating is often not so easy on the body. Full transparency: New meditators who come to join us for a retreat or as a new monk experience some form of physical discomfort about 98 percent of the time. This is just a reality of sitting still for extended periods of time.

But the first piece of good news is that you don't have to meditate long at all to start out. And the second piece of good news is that there are two main things that you can do to effectively create and maintain physical comfort:

    I. *Adopt a sitting position conducive to comfort*
    II. *Adjust or stretch the body*

Sitting Position

The first key area to focus on when establishing physical comfort is the way that you position your body when sitting for meditation. There are quite a few ways to do this. And it is important to note that one position is not inherently better than another. For simplicity and brevity's sake, this section will certainly not cover every single sitting arrangement out there.

So just keep in mind that the information found within the coming section is merely a framework to help you start experimenting. You don't have to rigidly adhere to the following advice. Through trial, error, and adjustment, you will discover a position that works best for your own body and mind.

So with that disclaimer in place, let's move on to the various areas that you can focus on when finding such a position. We can break up sitting position into a few different categories of focus as follows:

I. What You Sit On
II. Pelvic Alignment
III. Leg Positioning
IV. Back and Hand Positioning

What You Sit On

Let's start off with what you sit on. The most common arrangement is sitting on the ground cross-legged on a cushion of some sort. If you would like, you can look into buying a meditation cushion that is designed specifically for this purpose.

However, since there are so many options out there, we don't want the stress of picking one to keep you from starting your practice. So here are some household items that you can use to perform the function of a meditation cushion in case you don't already have one.

- Pillows (experiment with different sizes and softness)
- Couch cushions
- A few blankets
- A yoga mat
- Yoga blocks

We will go over some ideas on how to utilize and position these accessories in a moment.

But first, a note on chairs: Sometimes it is simply too painful for some people to sit on the ground. Just remember, comfort comes first. You can still meditate very well in a chair. So, go ahead and sit on one if your body is telling you to. If you want to work your way up (or down) to sitting on the ground, then you can do this gradually through doing some stretching and exercise.

Figure 21

But for now, you can experiment with sitting on different kinds of chairs to see what feels best. If you want to sit on a couch, you can give that a shot as well. But just be aware that the more comfortable your sitting area, the easier it is to drift off to sleep. For this reason, it is not recommended to meditate reclining or lying down, as it can be very difficult to maintain the proper level of awareness necessary for the mind to come to a standstill.

Pelvic Alignment

Once you figure out what you want to sit on, now it's time to adjust your body appropriately to promote proper circulation and reduce muscle fatigue and tension. We will address things in a bit of a strange order, but it will make sense once you read it.

First, let's start off with your pelvis. Many people will naturally sit with something that we call a posterior pelvic tilt. This basically means that the top of your pelvis is tilted backwards. You can look at Figure 22 to see an exaggerated version of what this looks like. You can also easily tell if you typically sit with this type of tilt by observing your sitting position now. Is your tailbone rounded underneath you and is there a hunch in your lower back? If yes, then you have a posterior pelvic tilt.

Figure 22

So how do we fix this? If you are standing right now for some reason (maybe you like to read standing up—I'm not here to judge), go ahead and take a seat as you normally would either on the ground or on a chair depending on how you will sit for meditation.

Now, with a straight back, lean forward until your butt starts to lift off the ground. While you are still leaning forward, start "walking" your butt backwards away from your knees by lifting up one side and "stepping" backwards. Repeat this a few times on each side.

Once you've taken a few "steps" backwards, lean back to your typical upright sitting posture.

Figure 23

You should already feel a bit more aligned and have a similar posture to the meditator in Figure 23. It's as if your sit bones—the ones at the bottom of your pelvis that you sit on—plug gently into whatever seat you have chosen. Just be mindful not to tilt too far in the opposite direction, as this will lead to a significant arch in the lower back as seen in Figure 24. This would create what we call an anterior pelvic tilt, which places strain on the lower back muscles.

Figure 24

So try to settle somewhere in the middle of overarching and hunching your lower back to arrive at a neutral lower spine alignment. This is the proper base for good posture both when sitting and standing.

Once you establish this neutral spine alignment, then it is often helpful to have some sort of cushion or blanket underneath your tailbone to provide some elevation and support. We will discuss this in more detail in a moment, but just know that this type of support often helps this pelvic alignment feel more effortless and devoid of bodily tension.

Leg Positioning

Now let's address your legs. If you are sitting on the ground, there is a pretty good chance you just naturally sat down "crisscross applesauce" like children often do. However, this sitting arrangement, as seen in Figure 25, is not ideal for meditation.

Figure 25

The main reason is because the contact of your shins on the top of your foot and heel will very often pinch a nerve and cause your feet to fall asleep after a short period of time.

The main goals of our leg positioning is to create a stable base, avoid pinching any nerves, promote proper circulation, and reduce strain on certain joints or muscles so that you can sit still without pain for as long as possible.

With this in mind, there are two main options that I would suggest. You can experiment to figure out which one works better for you. The first is called the half-lotus position where you put your right leg on top of your left leg as shown in Figure 26.

Figure 26

As always, you can make some slight adjustments to adopt a different variation that might feel more comfortable for you. Perhaps it feels better to place the right foot on the thigh closer to the left hip. Or maybe it feels better to position the foot more towards the knee. Maybe you actually like the left over the right. I could keep going on about various adjustments that you could make to the half-lotus posture. But I think you get the point; you don't have to look exactly like the photo. Adjust to find what works for you.

But maybe the leg positioning of the half-lotus posture just doesn't feel so comfortable regardless of the adjustments you make. Sometimes this sitting posture can feel a bit unbalanced and can create tension in the right hip, lower back, or ankle.

So another way to sit would be with the right in front of the left in the Burmese posture, as is shown in Figure 27. In this position, you place one leg in front of the other and both legs are flush against the ground. Again, just as with the previous posture, adjust as necessary and don't stress if you don't look exactly like the illustration.

Figure 27

However, let's address a fact you may have already discovered by trying to sit in either of these two recommended positions: It requires a fair bit of flexibility, especially in the hips. Perhaps when you try to sit like this your knees are way up in the air. Don't worry. There are things we can do to fix this problematic sitting position.

The reason it is problematic is because when your knees are suspended in the air like Figure 28, then it will put a tremendous amount of pressure on your ankles, knees, and hips. This, in turn, will create tension all throughout your body.

Figure 28

So, what we want to do to reduce this strain is create more contact with a surface to spread that pressure out over a larger area. Now remember those pillows and blankets that I told you to get earlier? Well, here is where they come into play.

The first thing you can do is lean forward and insert a pillow or rolled-up blanket underneath your tailbone or butt to elevate your hips before leaning back again into the properly aligned, neutral pelvic position that we talked about in the previous subsection. The general idea here is that your knees will be lower in relation to your hips. This will alleviate the strain you feel in both areas. If your legs are already relatively close to the floor, then you might only need a very slight amount of elevation to give you the extra angle you need to achieve full contact.

Figure 29

You can experiment with the thickness, firmness, and position of this pillow or blanket. Some people just need a little wedge under the tailbone. Others need to create a two-foot-tall super-booster seat. Whatever works for you is what is best.

If your legs are still off of the ground, the next thing you can do to create more contact with a surface is to use some pillows or rolled-up blankets to bolster up your knees.

Figure 30

Figure 30 gives you an idea of how you can position this extra support. Again, you can experiment with whatever accessories are most comfortable and supportive.

At the end of finding things to fortify yourself while sitting, you may have just crafted a pretty impressive pillow fort for yourself. And that's completely ok. After all, pillow forts are awesome! So don't be shy and just keep experimenting until you find the accessories that help you feel most comfortable while sitting.

Figure 31

For brevity's sake, we won't get into any details about this arrangement, but you are also welcome to research "meditation stools" if you want to try a different on-the-ground sitting position entirely.

If none of these things seem helpful or you just prefer to sit in a chair, then please do so. If you need to put a couch cushion or some rolled-up blankets under your feet to help them rest at a more comfortable height, then that can be a helpful adjustment to make for the chair meditators.

Lastly, we will cover the way that you can position your back and your hands. If you would like some back support, you are welcome to lean against a wall, a couch, a seat back, or any other surface to help keep you propped up. But just be aware that back rests make it easier to fall asleep. So it is best to maintain the pelvic alignment that we already addressed and not lounge or lean into the backrest too much to avoid sleepiness. If you want, you can put a pillow in between your lower back and the backrest in question if you find the extra support helpful.

Figure 32

Regarding your upper back, it is helpful to apply a slight activation between your shoulder blades so that your shoulders do not slouch or droop forward, leading to tension in the upper back, neck, and shoulders. What you can do to help avoid this is to imagine a string in between both of your shoulder blades that is pulling them together ever so slightly. This will help you stay broad and open across the chest.

But, of course, we also want to avoid overarching by cranking the shoulders back too far. What we are after is a middle way between an overarch and a slouch. Sidenote: It is very natural for this shoulder positioning to slacken as you relax into your meditation, so you do not need to be too serious or rigid in regards to maintaining this position. Just use it as a starting place and know that it can help to avoid muscular tension.

Now, while maintaining this back position, rest your hands ever so slightly in your lap. Sometimes, people will notice that this position pulls their shoulders downwards into a slouch. So what you can do is rest a pillow or blanket on your lap so that your hands can rest at a comfortable height to avoid a slouching posture. See Figure 33 for an idea of what this might look like.

Figure 33

The way that you place your hands could be a number of ways. First would be placing the right hand on top of your left palm with your right index finger touching the tip of your left thumb. But if this is not comfortable, you can adopt any other variation that you like.

Figure 34

Maybe you like bringing the thumbs together at the top. Maybe you like to have your hands stretched out onto your knees or thighs with your palms facing up. Or facing down. Again, it is all about what is most comfortable for you. So just experiment until you find what works best.

Countermeasures to Physical Tension

With all of those elements of sitting posture in place, you would expect your body to be completely at ease and pain free at all times, right? Well . . . unfortunately, that's typically not quite the reality with meditation. Even if you do manage to settle into an appropriate sitting position via the guidance provided in the previous subsection, it is still likely that you will experience some form of physical tension.

As we said earlier, this is very common for new meditators. Your body will likely require a certain time period to get used to sitting motionless. But, with that being said, there are a few things that you can do to reduce physical tension when it happens to arise.

If your body starts to ache during meditation, then the first thing you can do is simply notice it with a neutral attention. You can softly rest your awareness on this area of discomfort and use it as your new meditation tool. Or, after neutrally noticing the ache, you can gently reapply your mind to the meditation tool of your choice. Sometimes—much to the amazement of new meditators—the pain can just disappear after a short period of this neutral attention. Itches can also often disappear if we just notice them neutrally like this, so you can also try this approach in the event that an itch arises while meditating.

But there can also be times when your attention keeps getting pulled away from the meditation tool and back to that area of ever-increasing pain. Some other forms of meditation practice may just say to sit through it. And this can eventually lead to an overcoming of the pain once the mind surrenders and detaches from it, thus becoming more still.

But this can also be a very long and unenjoyable process. And we want you to enjoy, not suffer through, your meditation. So for this approach, comfort is the priority. If you experience persistent pain that doesn't dissipate after observing it or your chosen meditation tool calmly, it is best to simply adjust your body in a slow and mindful way.

If you move very intentionally, this adjustment can be made without a break in the continuity of your meditation. Moving your body with the mentality that you are still meditating during the entire adjustment can effectively allow you to reduce the discomfort while maintaining the stillness of your mind.

So again, your first options are to just observe the ache neutrally or place the mind back on the meditation tool instead of reacting abruptly with an immediate adjustment. But if you find that the pain gets worse and the mind cannot maintain a relaxed focus, then simply make a mindful adjustment in the way explained above.

Outside of Session – Stretch or Exercise

Another option to reduce physical tension would be to put in just a little bit of time outside of your meditation session to do some yoga, stretching, or exercise. These activities can be very helpful to promote proper circulation, release tension, and build the strength and flexibility necessary to meditate without pain. Then maybe eventually you won't need a pillow fort to meditate comfortably. ;) But, of course, I'm not trying to shame the pillow fort meditators. If it helps, keep doing your thing!

Although this is not 100 percent necessary, practices to relax or invigorate the physical body are definitely recommended. It is especially important if your aim is to progressively lengthen your meditation sessions over time. Doing some type of exercise or spiritual movement practice like yoga or Qigong either right before your meditation or sometime during the day can help tremendously to prepare your body to assume a comfortable sitting position. Then, when the body is adequately at ease, the mind can sink into a state of comfort more effortlessly.

Mental Comfort

Now we move on to the second half of Pillar One: mental comfort. In order to establish the mental comfort conducive to stillness of mind, we should ensure that:

1) we close our eyes softly and keep the muscles of our eyes and face relaxed;
2) the meditation tool that we are using feels easy, natural, and calming; and
3) we continuously maintain a mental state of neutrality and contentment.

Before we get into the first objective, let's make a quick note about the second objective. Using a tool that feels easy, natural, and calming is something that we already touched on quite a bit in the previous chapter where we discussed three different tools for meditation. So it isn't necessary to dedicate an entire subsection of this chapter to covering it again in much depth. But just as a quick review, the three tools discussed were: visualization, a mantra, and the center of the body. Again, these are just tools to reach stillness. If you have another tool that you are more confident with that is effective at stilling the mind, then you can use that as well.

But regardless of the tool you choose, the only question you should ask yourself to check if "the puppy in your mind" enjoys this tool is: Does the method that I'm using feel easy, calming, and natural? If the answer is no, then simply adjust your approach or switch the method until you discover a tool that fulfills these three requirements. If the answer is yes, don't change a thing. Just keep doing what you are doing. You are already on the correct path.

If you would like to review the way in which you can easily and naturally apply each tool in more detail, then you can look back at the previous chapter. So with that quick recap, let's get into the importance of objective number one.

Relax Your Eyes and Close Them Softly

This first objective is also a topic that we covered lightly in a few of the previous sections. However, it will be very helpful to provide you with some further details on this very crucial aspect of the practice. Now it might seem strange that "relaxing your eyes and closing them softly" is under the category of mental instead of physical comfort. After all, our eyes, eyelids, and the muscles in our face are parts of our physical body. But this topic has landed in this section to emphasize the very direct correlation that it has to the level of mental comfort we experience while meditating. We could even go so far as to say that the way in which we close our eyes sets the tone for our entire meditation.

Why is this? Well, we humans are very visual creatures. Our eyes are typically bombarded by an incredible amount of stimulation throughout the day. Whether we are staring at one of our electronic devices for hours on end, focusing on mountains of paperwork, or just scanning our environment as we go about our other daily tasks, our eyes are often extremely active and overburdened. This can lead to a lot of fatigue, tension, and heaviness within and around the eyes and muscles of the face.

Given this reality, it is not uncommon for meditators to have a bad habit of closing their eyes too quickly and with too much pressure, thus bringing residual tension and heaviness from their day into their meditation. Not taking enough time to adequately relax and release any tension or heaviness in the muscles surrounding the eyes will often give rise to quite a bit of mental tension when meditating. Without adequate relaxation, it can also be quite easy to continue using our physical eyes instead of allowing them to rest once we close our eyes. We can—as we discussed in a previous chapter—use our eyes to forcefully visualize or look at the point or space where we wish to anchor the mind. And, to reiterate, this is an ineffective approach that we want to avoid.

So in order to set the proper conditions for mental comfort to arise, you should take extra care to relax your eyes and close them as softly as possible each time you meditate. One way you can relax your eyes before closing them is to rub your hands together to generate some heat before placing your palms over your eyes for a few moments. You can repeat this a few times to allow the heat from your palms to relax and release some tension in and around your eyes. Another easy trick for further relaxation is to lightly massage your temples and your eyebrows.

Beyond these two very mechanical methods, a more passive and subtle way to relax your eyes before closing them would be to find a focal point in front of you at whatever height or distance feels most comfortable. You can then spend a little bit of time with your eyes open, allowing your gaze to relax, similar to how your gaze softens and unfocuses when you stare off into space while daydreaming. As you softly gaze in this way, you can even connect with your meditation tool as your eyes continue to relax and your mind starts to settle. Once your eyes feel adequately comfortable, it is almost as if they will want to close on their own.

At this point, simply close your eyes as softly and as gently as possible. Close them in much the same way you would when you are about to fall asleep. Close them so softly that it is almost as if your eyelids are barely even touching. Release all pressure and tension. Again, this will set a very soft and gentle tone for your meditation and help you establish the mental comfort necessary for stillness to arise.

Figure 35

Finally, if at any point during your practice you feel strain, pressure, heaviness, or tension within the eyes, then you can simply relax the muscles in and around your eyes, forehead, and face. Then just reapply your awareness more softly to the meditation tool in the way that we will discuss in an upcoming section about "placement of the mind." Adjusting in this way can be very effective at reestablishing mental comfort and overcoming not only mental tension but mind wandering as well.

Contentment & Neutrality Is Key

The final part of mental comfort that we want to establish and maintain is a feeling of contentment and neutrality.

Instead of looking for, wanting, or expecting results, we simply allow ourselves to sit with the most content and neutral state of mind possible. We are not trying to manufacture or search for a good feeling. Rather, when you allow your mind to simply be content—resting in a feeling that is not necessarily good or bad but just neutral—the feeling of comfort, inner peace, and stillness will arise on its own.

The following quote is a very telling phrase that illustrates the power of contentment quite accurately; "When you want nothing, you will get everything." Or said in another way: When you don't want anything, you already have everything you need.

This state of mind is something to be cultivated. It doesn't quite fit with the conventional wisdom of the physical world, where setting goals, pushing, and achieving accolades reigns supreme. The hustle culture promoted by our capitalist societies is quite opposite to the quote above. However, in the spiritual world, the rules are not quite the same as the physical world.

In the physical world, the more you push, work hard, and compete, the more you achieve. Effort and striving leads to results. But in the spiritual world, intense effort and striving leads to nothing but frustration.

When it comes to meditation, effort takes the form of becoming disciplined enough to show up on the mat every day. But once you close your eyes, you can only achieve genuine stillness of mind by letting go of desire and striving entirely. Minimize effort. Remain content and neutral. This is the key to making progress in meditation.

We establish such a mind state by not taking ourselves so seriously. We are patient and kind in the face of obstacles. We just show up on the mat, and whatever arises once we sit, we meet it with a sense of:

"I am completely ok with every aspect of the present moment. There is nothing more that I want. I am ok if my meditation does not go deeper than this. There is nothing about this moment that is worth getting frustrated about. I will remain accepting and patient in the face of any obstacles that arise—from my mind or the world around me—when meditating."

These statements reflect a mind that is not grasping at what its preferences are. It is a mind that is fully content and neutral. If you can truly grasp and apply the essence of these statements, it could save you weeks, months, or even years of frustration in your practice. In fact, I encourage you to go back now and read them again.

This content and neutral mindstate that we are elaborating on is a critical component to arriving at stillness. What we do is establish this state of mind and simply wait. We wait without expectation. We wait without anticipation. We aren't seeking to achieve anything. We just approach each session as if we are just resting the mind. Taking a little vacation. No pressure. No goals. Nothing. We don't aim for a good experience, just a neutral one.

If the mind wanders to the past or plans of the future, we notice that neutrally. If we fall asleep, upon awakening, we notice that neutrally. If our mind feels peaceful and then our dog barks, breaking us out of the stillness, we notice that neutrally as well.

And even if some pleasurable sensation accompanied by happiness and bliss shows up in our meditation, we also just continue to observe it very neutrally. It is extremely common for meditators of all experience levels to get excited when a new, enjoyable experience arises as a result of the mind becoming still. Oftentimes the ego will come in at this point and "step on the gas" in an attempt to push deeper into the inner experience. We grasp at the sensation. We try to analyze what it means, wondering, "Is this enlightenment!?"

But this mental activity simply causes the mind to be disturbed from its state of stillness. And since the stillness—which arises from letting go of effort—was the reason that this experience arose in the first place, it will naturally just disappear. So the proper way to progress and reach deeper levels of stillness when an enjoyable inner experience arises is to simply observe what is present in a very detached and neutral way. Calmly bring the mind back from its state of excitement, grasping, and wondering. Reestablish that neutrality of mind. And simply allow the inner experience to unfold without any interference on your part. This is, of course, easier said than done. But with practice, you will be able to maintain neutrality in the face of these experiences that initially excite the mind.

So to reiterate: No matter what arises—whether a good or bad, positive or negative, pleasurable or unpleasurable experience—we always just calmly detach from any emotions that pop up and return to a neutral observation of the present moment. In this way, we cultivate neutrality and contentment. With neutrality and contentment, we already have everything we need to succeed in the meditative path.

Awareness

The next key pillar necessary for stillness of mind is maintaining the proper level of awareness. For the first pillar, we establish comfort of body and mind. Essentially, we try to get to a point where we feel so comfortable, physically and mentally, that we could easily just drift off to sleep.

But we don't actually want to lose consciousness. Otherwise, you are just taking a nap instead of meditating. And if this happens to you . . . well, at least it shows that you have the first half of the equation down really well.

That sounds a bit like a joke. But, seriously, the mental state of a mind about to fall asleep is actually the proper mental state for stillness of mind to arise. But instead of slipping into that unconscious state, you maintain a gentle awareness.

This is where the three meditation tools that we discussed come into play. A meditation tool not only helps prevent the mind from wandering away to various thoughts; it also helps to keep the mind from falling asleep. So once we establish comfort of body and mind, a slight attention on a meditation tool helps us discover the proper balance for stillness to arise.

Placement of the Mind

When resting our awareness on the meditation tool in question, the effort that we use should be very minimal. To illustrate the ideal level of effort required to place the mind properly, we can make an analogy.

The placement of the mind should be as gentle as a bird's feather slowly floating down from the sky to land on the surface of a completely still pond without even causing a single ripple on the surface of the water.

Figure 36

And this is why we have to use a method that feels natural and easy for us to maintain our attention on: Because the proper place-ment of the mind requires subtlety, almost as if you are not even focusing at all. We want to place an effort that lies somewhere in between focusing and not focusing. It is a very soft and minimal kind of attention. This is the sweet spot that we are aiming for when placing the mind on a meditation tool.

But, of course, when trying to hone in on this very delicate balance, there will be times when you apply too much effort and other times when you don't apply enough. Too much effort can lead to both mental and physical tension. Too little can lead to the mind wandering away or drifting off into sleepiness.

But again, as we said before, all of these imbalances are very natural and to be expected. So simply be patient with yourself and gently reconnect your awareness to the meditation tool with this light "feather's touch" each time that you experience any imbalance.

In the beginning, and perhaps for quite a while, you will have to do this very frequently. Perhaps as much as ten, twenty, or fifty times in just a ten-minute session. This is just the reality of meditation. So, be kind and patient with yourself when this happens. Sure enough, if you apply these principles every day in meditation, bit by bit your mind will familiarize itself with this subtle touch and achieve a deeper, more stable stillness of mind.

A VISUAL SUMMARY
OF HOW TO MEDITATE

So with all of that information, it will be helpful for you to have a tool that helps you put all the pieces together so you can see the big picture of meditation at a glance. Instead of just a written summary of the meditation theory, the infographic representation that follows will help you quickly reconnect with the know-how covered in Part II of this book. At any point when you need to refresh yourself on the steps to achieve stillness, you can revisit this infographic that elaborates on the key points of the two pillars of stillness. You can also visit our website via the QR code or link provided below to access a printable version of this infographic.

QR code and link to access printable infographic
https://nickkeomahavong.com/meditation-1

COMFORT

Physical

Adjust the Body
Before Session

Exercise

Yoga

STRETCH

Mindfully Adjust
During Session

Not reactive,
Not pushing
though
pain...
just...

Maintain continuity of stillness while adjusting

Posture

Comfy Seat

Neutral Pelvis

Leg Support

Comfy Hands

Mental

Relax your eyes & Close them softly

Stay Content & Neutral

SHOULD FEEL

EASY NATURAL & CALMING

Go with the flow

AWARENESS

Tools	Placement

Visualization

"How you feel is more important than what you see"

Mantra

"A calming phrase"

The Center

"Awareness anchored in a point or a space"

A Feather's Touch

"Not too hard"
"Not too soft"

Continuously Reconnect

"Be kind and patient with yourself"

PART III:
LET'S GET STARTED

CHAPTER 5

ESTABLISHING
A DAILY PRACTICE

Now we have arrived at the most important part of this book: sitting for meditation. Hopefully, the aim to keep the conceptual part as bare-bones as possible has proven effective and your brain is not fried by this point. Oftentimes, people get stuck halfway through a book and never finish due to a surplus of nonessential information. If you got to this point, then congratulations! You're not one of those people. Give yourself a pat on the back. 'Tis a job well done.

But now it's time to put the theory aside and get to work. It's like going to the gym. You can spend time figuring out the right shoes to wear, which gym to get a membership at, what exercises you will do, and which pre-workout will give you the best pump . . . but to be honest, these things can just become procrastination disguised as productivity. You didn't *really* do anything yet. What is actually necessary is just showing up at the gym and starting to exercise. If you can't even show up, then there is nothing else to talk about.

Ultimately, meditation, like exercising, is an experiential journey, not a conceptual one. You must learn by doing. Then you can make adjustments along the way once you have something tangible to work with. And the key, as this book has repeated like a broken record up to this point, is building a *daily* practice. This is emphasized and reiterated for a reason. So, before we get into the practical steps of your action plan, let's hammer this concept home one last time.

The Importance of Daily Consistency

The first time that I became a monk in Thailand, I went through a rigorous one-month program where we would meditate for at least four to six hours per day and sometimes even more on top of our other monastic training. At the end of the program, many of my friends excitedly claimed that they would maintain this practice or scale down just a little bit to two hours per day once they made it back home. This mentality is also very common after people come back from an intensive meditation retreat.

But, most of the time, this habit doesn't last very long. I have heard so many stories of such people dropping off after a couple of months or even as little as a few weeks. Afterwards, they practice very irregularly or sometimes not at all.

For me, I knew that a daily practice was the key to incorporating meditation into my life in a sustainable way. So, I swallowed my pride and aimed low. How low? Five minutes a day. Just that. However, I was not only going to do this for thirty days; I made a strong commitment to keep this up for the next 365 days. For the next year, I would not let a single day go by without getting in those five minutes.

There were some days when I was extremely exhausted after a full day of work as a lead therapist at a foster home, multiple hours of dance practice, and long hours of sitting in LA traffic. I would collapse into bed at around one a.m. completely spent. And just as I was about to drift off to sleep—all of a sudden—I would remember, "Oh mannnn . . . I haven't meditated yet today."

I would groan as I got out of bed and sat my butt down for a sleepy five-minute session. But once that five minutes was up, I got back into my bed and passed out with a smile on my face. I would sleep soundly, knowing that "today, despite the resistance and how easy it would have been to just brush it off, I kept my word to myself. And *THAT* is something to be proud of."

There were some days that I meditated for more than that. I would sometimes sit for fifteen minutes, thirty minutes, and some days a little more. But I didn't get overconfident and raise my goal. Nope. Not yet. I kept my goal at five minutes as a bare minimum for the first 365 days.

Then, after that first year of meditation with my consistency thoroughly proven, I upped it to fifteen minutes for the next 365 days. Then, after that year, I upped it to thirty minutes. Over time, I found my rhythm. My muscles adjusted. My hips opened up. My mind settled. I overcame obstacles. I became more invested. I became . . . a true practitioner. But I started out small, because I knew the importance of setting myself up for success and following through on my commitments.

So, my advice to you? Approach this new practice with sustainability in mind. Start small and humble. Don't try to run before you can crawl. Slowly, over time, you can work up to thirty minutes, an hour, or maybe even more per day. But in the beginning of your meditation practice, slow and steady will win the race. And with the steps outlined in the next section, I *know* you will succeed in creating a strong foundation that will take you to whatever heights you dare to imagine for yourself. So, let's not waste any more time and get into it, shall we?

Action Plan to Get Started

So hopefully the conceptual part of this book has been easy *reading*, and now you feel confident and ready to start *doing*. If you don't, let me reassure you—you can do it! See? I even put in an exclamation point to express my conviction and belief in your capabilities. :)

So, how do you start? Here is a list of the essential commitments and decisions to make with some bonus recommended steps at the end:

1) Commit to sitting every single day.
2) Pick a minimum length of time that you can commit to every day.
3) Commit to at least a month, and ideally a year, of this practice.
4) Pick a time of day that is most convenient for you to meditate.
5) Pick a place to meditate.
6) Pick something to sit on—a chair, mat, blankets/ pillows, etc.
7) Pick a meditation style—silent, guided, or some

form of background noise. (*Visit the link in the footnote to access some meditation playlists and other resources that we have created*)[1]

8) Close your eyes and meditate.

9) (*Recommended but not mandatory*) Cross today off on your meditation habit tracker.

10) (*Recommended but not mandatory*) Make an entry in your meditation journal.

11) (*Recommended but not mandatory*) Chat with your accountability partner to either motivate, support, get feedback, or just discuss your meditation journey together. (*See the "Accountability Resources" section for more ideas about how to find and work with an accountability partner and to reference other beneficial accountability resources*)

Step 1, *making a commitment to sit every single day*, is the first step for a reason. Meditation must become a *daily habit* that is just as automatic as showering, brushing your teeth, eating, and sleeping. It is not something extra. It is not something you *find* the time for; it is something you *make* the time for. No matter how busy the day gets, we want to train ourselves in such a way that meditation is added to our list of nonnegotiable habits. It is a necessity for overall health of body and mind. So the frequency of meditating every day, seven days a week, is the first commitment you simply must make if you want to be successful in meditation. Commit to this and everything else will follow.

---

1 https://nickkeomahavong.com/meditation-1

Step 2, *pick a minimum length of time that you can commit to every day*, acknowledges the fact that people are busy. Not everybody can commit to thirty minutes right off the bat. Maybe twenty or fifteen minutes is also too much for you. Maybe ten is even pushing it.

Perhaps you are a medical student working two part-time jobs in between classes to pay the rent. Maybe you are a corporate executive with 76,534 employees that you must manage. Or perhaps you are a mother of seventeen children all under the age of ten. The truth is, each of these people can and should meditate. And so can and should you. The question is: How long is realistic and sustainable?

If ten minutes even seems like too big of a number, just commit to five minutes. You shouldn't go any shorter than this. Five minutes is the bare minimum amount of time necessary to instill a truly beneficial and sustainable habit. And you can do that for sure, no matter what your schedule or responsibilities are. Even if you are just dozing off during those five minutes, no worries! Remember that quality is secondary.

So set your goal with humility and the proper understanding of what we are aiming for: a daily habit. The key to succeeding in this is starting out small. Don't allow the smallness of the number of minutes you commit to cause you to overlook the significance of this commitment. You can always do more than this number on any given day. If you do, great! Bonus minutes! But your goal is to not let a day go by when you don't hit that minimum.

So setting a very modest goal does not equate to you being undisciplined or weak. It is simply a tactful approach that ensures you aren't setting yourself up for failure, disappointment, or stress from setting the bar too high. As the old adage goes, a meditation practice is a marathon, not a sprint. We are looking for sustainability. So, this technique of setting a modest goal helps us to achieve this.

Step 3, *committing to a month (at least)—or ideally a year—of this practice*, is the final essential commitment that you need to make in order to successfully implement a sustainable daily habit. Thirty days is a bare minimum. But, honestly, making a year-long commitment is much better.

By this point, hopefully you understand that meditation is not a trend or a fad. It's not a thirty-day detox. It is a basic human need that we have to do every day just like showering the body. You don't just shower daily for thirty days and then say, "Welp, that should be about enough! Now I can go back to smelling like a farm animal!"

Meditation is the same. If we value our mental health, the ability to see things clearly, and maintaining a good quality of life, then we must meditate every day. If you equip yourself with this type of long-term mentality, then you will *absolutely* succeed.

Step 4, *picking a time of day that is most convenient for you to meditate*, acknowledges the fact that everybody's disposition and situation is vastly different. Some people are *not* morning people. They perpetually wake up on the wrong side of bed. So, maybe morning is not the best time to meditate for such individuals. Other people are exhausted by the time the night rolls around, so maybe *that* time isn't ideal for *them*. Some people are simply too busy at both of these time periods but can squeeze in a quick sitting session in their car before they go back into work during their lunch break.

You know you and your situation best. So, it is up to you to decide which time of day is appropriate for your sitting session given your unique set of circumstances. Don't overthink this one. Just pick a time and then try it out. If it ends up not being such a convenient or appropriate time, then just try a new one.

One tip that I will share, however, is that getting in your meditation minutes right after you wake up might help you more effortlessly implement this daily habit into your life. There are a couple of reasons for this. Firstly, once you get it finished as soon as you wake up, it isn't hanging over your head as an unfinished task all day long. If things get a bit hectic during your day, it becomes easier to just blow off your meditation minutes or forget about them entirely.

Morning meditation can also set a good tone for the rest of your day as you take a moment to get still before tackling your long to-do list. And finally, it provides you with a psychological boost similar to the one you get from making your bed first thing every morning. You just start the day off with a small win. You complete a task that brings a bit more inner peace and order to your life. Then you can walk out the door carrying that proud feeling that you get when you triumphantly put a checkmark next to today's date on your meditation calendar (a tool that we will cover in the next section).

But, of course, don't allow these notions to force yourself to meditate in the morning if you happen to be someone who is a cranky zombie until about an hour into the day. Again, adjust according to what works for you.

Step 5, *picking a place to meditate*, is going to be quite dependent on your schedule and the time of day that you chose in the previous step. If, during that time, you happen to be at home, then figure out which place will work best for you. If it is a space in your room, then you can clean, declutter, and rearrange some things to make the environment more relaxing. You might decide to put up a picture of an inspirational figure. You could even arrange some candles, some incense, or an altar. Feel free to get creative.

If it happens to be in your car on your lunch break, then maybe you can park in a shady spot with a nice view. If it is outside, feel free to buy a meditation mosquito net (if they happen to be a problem at that time in your location). You can take a few measures to help make your meditation space more comfortable, but try to avoid getting caught up for too long at this stage. The space doesn't have to be perfect to get started. You can always tweak it over time to be more inspiring for your practice.

Step 6, *picking something to sit on*, will also be quite dependent on what you decided on in the previous two steps. The first factor to consider is, of course, your physical comfort. So, if you simply do not have the flexibility to sit on the ground, experiment with various chairs to find what works best for you. Slowly, you can move down to the ground if it is your aim to work on flexibility. If not, then don't feel pressured to do so if a chair works well for you.

Regarding sitting on the ground, you can either take a look at the visual summary from the previous section or revisit the section about physical comfort to review some suggestions for finding a comfortable sitting position. Again, you don't need to spend too much time deciding what to sit on, because only after trying will you be able to figure out what works or does not work for your body.

Step 7, *picking a meditation style*, involves deciding if you want to meditate in silence or with some form of accompanying audio. If you want to meditate in silence, then you can set a timer on your phone or use a video from my silent meditation playlist that has various lengths of time in silence with a bell at the end.

However, if you want to meditate with some form of audio in the background, whether that is guided meditations or nature sounds, then you have quite a few options at your disposal. To help you avoid feeling overwhelmed by all of the options out there, you can visit the link in the footnote below[2] for some options that we have compiled on our website, including YouTube playlists, audio files, and more.

If there tends to be noise in the surrounding area you choose for meditation, then using headphones or earbuds along with one of the resources found on the website can be very helpful to create a peaceful atmosphere for yourself despite noisy surroundings. Again, there is no need to get hung up at this stage. Simply try meditating in silence or with one of the resources above and adjust if it does not feel like such a suitable approach for you.

Step 8 *is to close your eyes softly and meditate!*

Steps 9 - 11 are either self-explanatory or discussed in one of the "Accountability Resources" sections after the conclusion (or in another book, for the case of meditation journaling) and so will not be covered in more detail here.

---

2 https://nickkeomahavong.com/meditation-1

With these decisions and commitments made, you are now ready to confidently begin your daily practice. Make sure to reference the accountability tools that follow the conclusion for some great interactive tools to help you implement this action plan and support you on your meditation journey!

CHAPTER 6

THE JOURNEY
TO INNER SPACE

Problems in Outer Space

So now you are fully equipped with the know-how, tools, and mentality to establish a daily practice. The theory that you have learned in this book constitutes the universal building blocks of meditation. And the action plan that you have just read in the previous section gives you the practical steps to integrate the theory into your life through direct experience. But before we wrap up this book and send you happily down the path to enlightenment, let's revisit a very important topic: suffering.

The world is very chaotic right now. There is no denying it. We, as a collective, are suffering more than ever before. Yes, there have been incredible tragedies such as mass famine and world wars in the past, but life in modern times is just a lot more complex than it was in any other era that has come before.

Not only do we have to contend with the issues present in our personal lives, those of our extended family, and our surrounding community or country at large, but we are now aware of and affected by problems that happen on the other side of the world almost instantaneously. In the age of information, we are hyper-aware of all of the ways in which the world is headed for—or already in—a state of disaster: socially, economically, environmentally, and so on.

For the longest time, we have been seeking to solve these problems via efforts in the outside world. Growth. Progress. Exploration. Discovery. Science. Technology. Advancement. More. Faster. Better. Farther. In many ways, these strides forward in the physical world have led to a higher standard of living for an incredibly large number of people. Medical expertise and practices have come leaps and bounds. Access to clean water and food has increased tremendously across the globe. The list goes on. But despite these increases in standard of living, we are still suffering more than ever before.

And the strange thing is, modern technologies now provide us with access to all of the philosophies, strategies, and solutions of the smartest and most influential individuals and leaders throughout all of recorded history. So, this begs the question: Why can't we apply this knowledge to overcome the issues we face? This bizarre predicament shows that we don't suffer from a lack of information. Rather, we suffer from a lack of wisdom.

One way wisdom could be defined is "knowledge in accordance with the true nature of things." Wisdom comes with the ability of knowing how to utilize information properly to problem-solve effectively. Ultimately, our predicament comes down to the fact that we are looking for the answers in all the wrong places.

Houston, We've Had a Problem

To illustrate a new approach that we can take to solving the world's most troubling issues, we can look towards one of the most amazing products of our technological advancements: space exploration. Let's look specifically at sending astronauts to the moon.

The journey to the moon is certainly a long one. It requires the combined efforts of the top experts in many different fields to successfully send a manned aircraft to the moon and bring the astronauts back home to Earth safely. Once the mission is underway, it requires two separate teams. (*I'm definitely oversimplifying this process for the sake of a brief analogy, so please excuse any technical inaccuracies.*) There, of course, must be one team of astronauts inside the space shuttle and then another team of various experts on the ground in Mission Control.

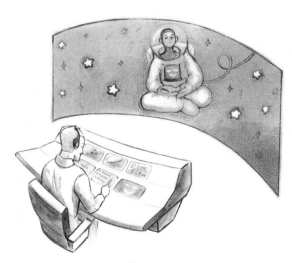

Figure 37

The Mission Control team has the responsibility of monitoring everything that goes on before, during, and after takeoff. Whether it's from movie scenes or from actual footage of real space missions, you have likely seen some depiction of the atmosphere inside Mission Control. Situations can be quite tense. The stakes are high. The headsets are on. And the engineers are all in front of computer screens with advanced mathematical equations on them.

Each individual in that room works together to observe the mission from all angles with utmost vigilance. They must remain in constant contact with the astronauts throughout the entire flight to help guide them safely through every step of their dangerous journey.

On one particular journey to the moon, Apollo 13, there was a serious issue. Everything seemed to be going well as the shuttle was gliding through space, making its way steadily towards its destination. The plan was to land on the moon the following morning. However, during some routine checks before retiring for bed that evening, the astronauts heard a large bang that sent shockwaves down the entire structure of the spacecraft. A sense of fear and uncertainty gripped the astronauts. Over the radio back on the ground in Texas, Mission Control received the famous message, "Houston, we've had a problem."

A faulty oxygen tank had exploded during a routine procedure and caused serious damage to multiple systems on the spacecraft. From that moment onwards, Mission Control and the astronauts aboard had to make clear-headed decisions to properly identify the issues at hand and implement their best solutions. Ultimately, the mission to land on the moon had to be aborted. The new mission: get the astronauts back to Earth alive.

Various teams at Mission Control had to make autonomous decisions. Everyone needed to know what to do and when. Time was of the essence. Oxygen was running low. Electricity had to be conserved. Simulations had to be run. Calculations had to be . . . calculated.

And each member of each team had to relay their findings to the appropriate people at the proper time. And during all of these high-pressure, high-stakes operations, it was of paramount importance that everyone remained calm. Emotions had to be placed to the wayside. If anyone succumbed to panic, people would die.

However, through immense cooperation and effort from many skilled individuals, all three of the astronauts who embarked on the Apollo 13 mission returned home safely. Mission control played an absolutely essential role in being able to guide those three men out of imminent doom and back to Earth . . . where they all lived happily ever after.

Take Back Mission Control

Now, you might be thinking, "Cool story . . . but I'm still wondering why I'm getting a history lesson about space in a meditation book." And fair enough. This story might seem a bit random. But, if we look at this Apollo 13 mission a bit more closely, it actually shares some very interesting parallels to our own life.

What was it that allowed the astronauts and Mission Control to effectively overcome the dire situation they found themselves in? Of course, their expertise was an essential factor. But in order to utilize those skills to problem solve effectively, they needed to observe things *neutrally*.

Why is this so crucial? Well, imagine if the moonbound astronauts relayed the message back to Mission Control in Houston that they've had a problem, and in response, they were met by a chorus of terrified screams and conflicting orders saying, "What? WHAT?! I HAVEN'T BEEN PAYING ATTENTION!! WHAT DO WE DO? FULL THRUST AHEAD! NO NO, TURN OFF THE ENGINES! HIT THE EJECT BUTTON! THEY'RE NOT GONNA MAKE IT!!! AHHHHHH!!" This certainly wouldn't be a very comforting, confidence-inspiring, or helpful response, to say the least.

When a crisis arises in a space mission, it requires everyone on the ground in Mission Control and each of the astronauts on the space shuttle to put their emotions aside, take a deep breath, and continue observing the issue neutrally. Once they observe the situation calmly, then they can see where the issues are and correct them quickly and effectively. They can respond to the situation wisely. We could say that a team such as this has extremely refined skills of observation. No amount of expertise would be able to compensate for lacking this state of calm in such a crisis situation.

So how does this relate to meditation and the problems we face in our own lives? Well, as we go throughout life, we interact with the world in "outer space," or—in other words—the physical world. We push for progress and productivity. We pursue education. We build relationships. We develop a career. We amass resources to provide for ourselves and the ones we love. And all along the way, we naturally run into a whole mess of problems.

Some of them are relatively minor. Others are downright life crises. Some affect only us. And others are global disasters. But one thing is for sure: We all must find our own ways of coping with such issues. Life is essentially a series of solving (or avoiding) problems.

But the (other) problem is, as we are out here expending all of our energy and focus in "outer space," most of us fail to realize that everyone in our own "inner Mission Control" has abandoned their post. And now that the problems are multiplied by the current state of our world, the flying is *very* dangerous. Houston . . . we've had *a lot* of problems! And we will *continue* to have a lot of problems if Houston can't get itself together.

Honestly, "getting Houston together" is one of the most beneficial gifts we can give to ourselves and those around us. Because this "inner Mission Control" is responsible for one of the greatest powers that we have as human beings: The power to choose how we respond to each and every situation that we face.

But all too many of us are underutilizing this incredible power by habitually reacting to life on autopilot and behaving like a puppet to our own cravings, aversions, and delusions. When we experience things that we like and want, it can often cause us to think, speak, and act unskillfully under the influence of greed. Conversely, when we experience things that we don't like and don't want, it can often cause us to think, speak, and act unskillfully under the influence of anger. And we craft many inaccurate views from a tainted perception colored by our conditioning, fluctuating emotional states, and delusional assumptions.

When there is little to no awareness of these thought, speech, and behavior patterns, we have no opportunity to intervene and change them. This is like having no "inner Mission Control" to utilize in order to give us feedback and guidance as we hurtle haphazardly through "outer space." Instead, a faulty autopilot software is running in our team's absence, causing us to stay unknowingly entrenched in these patterns that cause unnecessary suffering for ourselves and those around us.

But the good news is, you are now fully equipped to take your power back. By dedicating at least five minutes each day to closing your eyes and showering the mind, something amazing will start to happen. You will start to slowly staff that "inner Mission Control." The stillness you collect day by day will create a little breathing room between stimulus and response. Then, when a situation where you typically react impulsively arises, a new inner voice of purity from your "inner Mission Control" will arise as well.

This inner voice interrupts you right as you are about to give someone an earful with something along the lines of, "Wait . . . don't say that."

Figure 38

Or it tells you, "Hold on a second. Let's do something else," right as you are about to indulge in a bad habit. Or it snaps you out of a negative train of thought with the suggestion, "Maybe that actually isn't true."

In the tiniest of moments like these, you are able to break the cycle of your maladaptive patterns and make new choices. You are empowered to take a breath and gently redirect your mind towards staying rooted in stillness. And as you disengage from any emotions, cravings, and aversions that have arisen, you can observe things neutrally. You can see things more clearly. As a result, you can respond to that situation with wisdom instead of reacting with impulse.

Life is a continuous stream of these brief moments where small choices can make the biggest difference.

Although the effect of this choice may seem small at first, it can very quickly and deeply transform your life and the way you interact with the world when compounded over time. When we cultivate our skill of continuously bringing the mind back to a state of neutral observation through daily meditation, we have a fighting chance to carry that neutrality into our daily lives. The wiser choices we make as a result create more benefit and reduce more suffering for both ourselves and others around us.

But, of course, cultivating something means that it takes time and effort. This is why meditation is called a "practice." Because it takes repetition. And because you are practicing for *real* life. You are practicing and slowly building that ability to observe things in "outer space" neutrally.

At this very crucial turning point in history, meditation is no longer much of an option. In a time where so many external factors continuously contribute to the murkiness of our mental space, a daily shower for the mind is essential. In the age of a surplus of inaccurate, emotionally triggering information, clarity is a must. If you cannot *see* yourself, others, or the world around you clearly, you won't be able to see your own problems clearly. And as the world continues to shift and transform at a frightening pace, you will struggle to keep up. Adapting will be very difficult. And that is extremely dangerous—for you and everyone around you.

Enough is enough. You have been flying blind for too long. It's time to put in the work to properly man your station. It is time to bring your mind back home to where it can be calm and function effectively. You have the tools you need to succeed. You can do it. All that is left for you to do is to firmly make the decision that it's time to take back Mission Control. In order to effectively solve the world's biggest problems that we all face in "*outer* space," we, as a collective, must individually undertake the journey to "*inner* space."

People can often feel lost and hopeless in the face of modern calamities. They want to know how they can play their part in making the world a better place. Let me tell you confidently: *This* is where you start. It's not a grand public gesture that will gain you the praise and adoration of the masses. But this uncelebrated daily habit of cultivating stillness of mind will empower you to make wiser choices that will have positive ripple effects that are more powerful and far-reaching than we could ever measure or imagine.

As you undertake this inner journey and gain ever-deepening access to the reserves of that inner well, you will—as the serenity prayer suggests—continuously develop the serenity to accept the things you cannot change, the courage to change the things you can, and the wisdom to know the difference. Without these three virtues, we are all just stumbling around in the dark. But with them, everything is possible. With them, we, as a collective, can make those small, wise, moment-to-moment choices that can redirect our world that is hurtling through outer space towards a brighter destination.

I hope you understand the gravity of the situation now. And with the building blocks of meditation in your hands, I hope you are now confident that you can succeed in establishing a truly sustainable and transformative daily practice. *I* am confident that you can. Thanks for reading. Good luck on your journey. And I'll see you in the next book. Happy meditating, my friend.

ACCOUNTABILITY RESOURCES

Welcome to this final section full of extra resources to help you succeed in starting and progressing down this meditative path. Each one of these resources will have corresponding online content consisting of either printable templates to fill out or an online community that you can connect with. Please scan the QR code below or enter the link into your browser to visit these hubs of helpful information that will give you access to extra resources in addition to the ones referenced in the coming pages. We hope these resources enrich your spiritual journey. Enjoy!

 QR code and link for all of the printable templates on the following pages:
https://nickkeomahavong.com/meditation-1

TAKE A VOW AND MAKE IT OFFICIAL

After you have made all of the commitments from the action plan section, you can make them official by plugging them into the following template. Feel free to write directly in this book, design your own, or visit our website to print this template. If you decide to fill out a vow outside of this book, feel free to tape it to your mirror or in a prominent place where you will see it every single day. This will help keep you accountable for this life-changing practice and remind you of the importance of following through on your commitment.

I, _____, make a vow to . . .

Meditate seven days a week
For at least _____ **minutes every day**
For the next _____ **days.**

Start Date _____
Signature _____

MEDITATION
HABIT TRACKER

Another invaluable tool that will help you stay accountable and track your progress is a meditation habit tracker. The process of crossing off the days that you have completed your meditation is very satisfying. You get to see a physical representation of how far you have come and get to feel proud of yourself each day that you follow through on your commitment. Day by day, tick mark by tick mark, you build a stronger and stronger foundation. You feel more accomplished and motivated to continue. This process can be very fun and exciting, so enjoy!

The habit trackers that follow will give you a few ideas of different formats that you can utilize to help you track your progress. If you would like to download and print any of these habit trackers, then you can do so on our website.

HABIT TRACKER # 1

Daily goal: _____ minutes   Month of: _____

SUN	MON	TUE	WED	THU	FRI	SAT

Insights from this month

HABIT TRACKER # 2

Daily goal: _____ minutes   Start date: _____

S	M	T	W	T	F	S	Minutes meditated
○	○	○	○	○	○	○	_____
○	○	○	○	○	○	○	_____
○	○	○	○	○	○	○	_____
○	○	○	○	○	○	○	_____
○	○	○	○	○	○	○	_____
○	○	○	○	○	○	○	_____
○	○	○	○	○	○	○	_____

Total: _____

How do you feel after . . .

Week 1:   Week 4:   Week 7:

Week 2:   Week 5:

Week 3:   Week 6:

HABIT TRACKER # 3

January

S	M	T	W	T	F	S
						1
2	3	4	5	6	7	8
9	10	11	12	13	14	15
16	17	18	19	20	21	22
23	24	25	26	27	28	29
30	31					

February

S	M	T	W	T	F	S
		1	2	3	4	5
6	7	8	9	10	11	12
13	14	15	16	17	18	19
20	21	22	23	24	25	26
27	28					

March

S	M	T	W	T	F	S
		1	2	3	4	5
6	7	8	9	10	11	12
13	14	15	16	17	18	19
20	21	22	23	24	25	26
27	28	29	30	31		

April

S	M	T	W	T	F	S
					1	2
3	4	5	6	7	8	9
10	11	12	13	14	15	16
17	18	19	20	21	22	23
24	25	26	27	28	29	30

May

S	M	T	W	T	F	S
1	2	3	4	5	6	7
8	9	10	11	12	13	14
15	16	17	18	19	20	21
22	23	24	25	26	27	28
29	30	31				

June

S	M	T	W	T	F	S
			1	2	3	4
5	6	7	8	9	10	11
12	13	14	15	16	17	18
19	20	21	22	23	24	25
26	27	28	29	30		

July

S	M	T	W	T	F	S
					1	2
3	4	5	6	7	8	9
10	11	12	13	14	15	16
17	18	19	20	21	22	23
24	25	26	27	28	29	30
31						

August

S	M	T	W	T	F	S
	1	2	3	4	5	6
7	8	9	10	11	12	13
14	15	16	17	18	19	20
21	22	23	24	25	26	27
28	29	30	31			

September

S	M	T	W	T	F	S
				1	2	3
4	5	6	7	8	9	10
11	12	13	14	15	16	17
18	19	20	21	22	23	24
25	26	27	28	29	30	

October

S	M	T	W	T	F	S
						1
2	3	4	5	6	7	8
9	10	11	12	13	14	15
16	17	18	19	20	21	22
23	24	25	26	27	28	29
30	31					

November

S	M	T	W	T	F	S
		1	2	3	4	5
6	7	8	9	10	11	12
13	14	15	16	17	18	19
20	21	22	23	24	25	26
27	28	29	30			

December

S	M	T	W	T	F	S
				1	2	3
4	5	6	7	8	9	10
11	12	13	14	15	16	17
18	19	20	21	22	23	24
25	26	27	28	29	30	31

CLARIFY
YOUR WHY

Getting clear on the most powerful reasons why you want to create and maintain a meditation habit is a very beneficial exercise both at the beginning and along the way of your meditation journey. At first, there will most likely be some resistance and struggles as you seek to incorporate this behavior change into your daily life. And there will also likely be rough patches in your practice where you don't feel so motivated to sit. So having a one-page sheet of your deepest motivations for practicing can be an easy way to reconnect with a powerful source of internal motivation. It can help you persevere in the face of resistance.

So take some time now to brainstorm why you are incorporating meditation into your life. Maybe it's for the sake of overcoming anxiety or depression. Maybe you want to be more focused at work. More mentally present for the important people in your life. Increase your mental clarity to problem-solve more effectively. Or maybe you want to uproot the impurities in your mind and attain enlightenment.

Whatever the case may be, jot it down on the next page, on a separate piece of paper, or download and fill out the template from our website. Once you have a few powerful reasons, keep this in a prominent place where you can reconnect with that internal source of motivation to keep staying consistent in this transformative practice. Feel free to add more reasons to this list as you progress on your journey and experience new positive benefits in your life.

CLARIFY YOUR WHY

Why is a meditation practice important to you?

CONNECT WITH AN ACCOUNTABILITY PARTNER

Another incredibly powerful resource to support your journey is getting an accountability partner. Having an individual who is building a meditation habit alongside you greatly enriches your experience and is incredibly beneficial in many ways. It allows you to share this journey with another as you support each other through the ups, downs, and in-betweens of your practice.

If a friend or family member wants to go on this journey with you, then this section will give you some ideas on how to best support each other. But if none of your loved ones are up for the task, you can visit the link provided in the footnote where you can access a special post on our online Reddit community. This post is dedicated to helping those searching for an accountability partner connect with other spiritual seekers with the same intention. You can also browse the other meditation-related posts to share your journey with the larger online community. [1]

Ideas for accountability partners:
- Decide how often/when you will meet up/discuss your experiences.
- Share your goals with each other.

---

[1] https://nickkeomahavong.com/meditation-1

- Discuss the reasons why you both want to build this habit.
- Share inspirational words or quotes to motivate each other.
- Share/ask about techniques that have been effective.
- Share what things you have found are helpful to avoid in order to meditate more effectively.
- Share/ask about your favorite journaling formats or techniques.
- Share/ask what accessories/seats/locations have been helpful for your body and mind.
- Share/ask what time of day works best and why.
- Share/ask what things you do to prepare well for meditation.
- Share/ask what types of resources/apps/guided meditations have helped.

ENDING
CONTENT

ACKNOWLEDGMENTS

To our meditation masters, we could never hope to truly be able to express the depth of your wisdom fully. However, we humbly hope that our efforts have preserved the integrity of your teachings on this most sacred of subjects. Without your sacrifice, wisdom, dedication, vision, purity, loving kindness, compassion, and all of the other wholesome qualities that you embody, we would never have been able to live the monastic life with so much joy or have the opportunity to discover this bright inner light to share with the world. We could never fully repay our debt of gratitude but hope that our actions make you proud to have us as your sons in the Sangha. We are so grateful for your guidance and look forward to many more years of helping your vision of achieving world peace through inner peace become a reality. We rejoice in your immeasurable merit and share all of our merit with you.

To our teachers—Venerable Narongchai, Venerable Pawithai, Venerable Burin, our meditation teachers and tutors, and other spiritual mentors—we are eternally grateful for your support in creating a strong foundation for our monk life and for entrusting us with the freedom and responsibility of sharing the Dhamma in a way that we truly love. Thank you for believing in us and giving us the space to grow and mature.

To Venerable Tim Dhiranando: Your artwork is truly breathtaking and incredibly sacred. The love and care that you have put into your work shines through in the beauty of the illustrations and cover design. Your efforts will undoubtedly help so many individuals out there on their path of self-discovery find this true refuge of inner peace inside of themselves. Thank you for your dedication as well as your support and spiritual friendship. We are so proud to call you a brother and a close kalyanamitra.

To each of our families, we would like to express our deepest gratitude. If it weren't for your love and sacrifice throughout our lives, we would certainly not be where we are today. So much of what we do is to repay the large debt of gratitude we have for all that you have given us. We would like to share all our merit from this lifetime with you.

To Emmy Boonsakulcharoen, thank you for your help in designing the journal, some beautiful accountability resources, your expertise throughout this project, and for your support and faith in us. We rejoice in your merit!

To Stephanie Pailin Thiel, Thidarat Thaiyanon, and Puttamaporn Jittrawong, thank you for your generosity and expertise by helping with formatting the text and fine tuning the covers to be very sleek and aesthetic. We rejoice in your merit!

To all of our teachers, friends, monk brothers, previous work colleagues, supervisors, and clients: Thank you for all the support, guidance, and encouragement along the way. You all played a significant part in our journey that led to the creation of this book, so we hope you enjoyed the read and can benefit from the content. Stay tuned for the next one!

ABOUT THE AUTHORS
Venerable Nick Santacitto

Venerable Nick, previously a practicing psychotherapist, has been ordained as a Theravada Buddhist monk in Thailand since 2018. His books capture his unique perspective by interweaving the tools of the mental health world and the wisdom of Buddhism into simple and practical guides to healing. With a background as a YouTuber and a professional hip-hop dancer, Nick likes to keep it real and deliver his message to the reader with a refreshing, modern flavor. The directness of his writing cuts past the fluff and gets to the point in a way that is relatable and easy to connect with.

Nick has acquired a diverse range of professional experience in the mental health field over the past decade, including but not limited to: being the lead clinician at a foster home for over one hundred kids aged twelve to eighteen; being a program therapist at a drug treatment center in Malibu, California; being a bereavement counselor at a hospice; and being the founder and owner of his private practice, True Nature Counseling Center, in San Diego, California.

However, at the pinnacle of his professional success, Nick left it all behind to become a Buddhist monk in Thailand. He wanted to delve deeper into his own healing and become a more refined practitioner of the tools that he was teaching. As he fully focused his energy on becoming more deeply congruent and aligned with his true nature, his understanding of human suffering and how to heal it matured greatly. It is his highest mission to share this knowledge with others in order to help them discover their true nature and live their most authentic lives.

ABOUT THE AUTHORS
Venerable Michael Viradhammo

After discovering the healing power of Buddhism and meditation, Venerable Michael decided to abandon material pursuits, dropped out of university, paid back his loans, and went to ordain as a Buddhist monk in Thailand, where he has been a monk since 2017. After ordaining, Venerable Michael has spent much of his time teaching meditation and wisdom to travelers at the Pa Pae Meditation Retreat in Chiang Mai as well as teaching and mentoring men who become monks with the international ordination program.

He is also an avid writer and is pursuing his passion by cowriting books about practical wisdom to help readers overcome their suffering with his monk brother, Venerable Nick. By learning, applying, teaching, and writing Venerable Nick's unique perspective that bridges mental health with spiritual health, Venerable Michael is deeply dedicated to continuously aligning his life with his true nature and helping others do the same.

CONNECT WITH
THE AUTHORS

Visit Venerable Nick's website for a central place to access all of the projects that he has completed and is currently working on: https://nickkeomahavong.com/

Get a better feel for the broad range of topics, concepts, and stories that Venerable Nick has an interest in by visiting his YouTube channel: Nick Keomahavong.

Stay updated with any new resources, products, or other announcements by signing up for Venerable Nick's mailing list: tinyurl.com/nickkeomahavong

Join our online Reddit community where we keep the conversation going. This platform helps to foster strong spiritual friendships and instigate the discussion surrounding Venerable Nick's content. Come share your story: https://www.reddit.com/r/NickKeomahavong/

Printed in Great Britain
by Amazon

83031945R00088